We Believe in One True God

An Exposition of the Christology of the Syrian Orthodox Church through the Eucharistic Liturgy

Rev. Dr Joseph Varghese

© 2023 Rev. Dr Joseph Varghese

All rights reserved. No part of this publication may be reproduced, stored in a retrieval system, or transmitted, in any form or by any means, electronic, mechanical, photocopying, recording or otherwise, without the permission in writing from the Author.

ISBN: 978-1-961472-37-2

Edited and Published by:
Amazon Publishing Solutions
USA.

Printed by:
Amazon, USA.

Abstract

This study investigates the Christology of the Syrian Orthodox Church in terms of how it is expressed through the Fraction Rite of the Eucharistic liturgy. The development of liturgy overall is examined here with a particular emphasis on the liturgy of St. James, the non-Chalcedonian stance on Christology within certain geo-political situations, and the evolution of the liturgy over the centuries in the Syrian Orthodox Church. Included is the role of the *communicatio idiomatum* in defining the Person of Christ in the Antiochene and Alexandrian Schools. The study further details how the Syrian Orthodox Church professes its faith through the Eucharistic Liturgy. A close reading is given of the rubrics of the Eucharistic prayer including the Fraction Rite, along with an analysis of the prayers and hymns associated with the rite, in order to establish the theological connection between the *lex orandi* and the *lex credendi*. In many ways, the Fraction Rite is a microcosm of the Christological position of the Syrian Orthodox Church. In particular, the significance of the breaking of the sacramental bread into particles and the co-mingling, the use of leavened bread (which is peculiar to the Orthodox churches in general), the hymns which accompany these actions, and even the positions of the sacramental bread on the paten, are all ways in which the Syrian Eucharistic liturgy bespeaks that community's faith in the personhood of Christ.

Acknowledgements

It is not surprising that such kind of a work on history and belief could hardly have been written without a personal spiritual commitment and a strong upbringing in a faith which can traced back its history since the beginning of Christendom. I am very much indebted to the Holy Syrian Orthodox Church of Antioch through which I heard, learned and practiced my faith throughout my entire life. It has a profound role in my spiritual and faith development. First and foremost, I acknowledge to the Holy Syrian Orthodox Church, its Doctors, Fathers, Theologians and leaders who are all left an unperishable legacy and teachings on the Faith of the Holy Church and their work I used extensively as my primary and secondary sources of information. I acknowledge my allegiance to the Apostolic See of Antioch and 123rd successor of St. Peter, His Holiness Ignatius Ephrem 2nd, the Patriarch of the Syrian Orthodox Church of Antioch and all the East and all Metropolitans of the Holy Church. I would like to acknowledge Archbishop Titus Yeldho of the Malankara Archdiocese in North America, to whom I have requested to do a foreword for this book. I like to acknowledge Father Matthew S. Ernest, Academic Dean, Professor and Director of Liturgy at Saint Joseph's Seminary in Yonkers, New York for his valuable advice and guidance on my work on Christology in Liturgy during my master's degree program which is a pre-cursor of this book. I also acknowledge my family, friends and parishioners for their valuable prayers and support.

Finally, I acknowledge Zach Andrew, Senior Project manager of the Amazon Publishing Solutions and his entire editorial team for the great help in editing, designing and publishing this book.

MALANKARA ARCHDIOCESE
of the Syrian Orthodox Church in North America
(Under the Holy Apostolic Throne of Antioch and All the East)

Archbishop Mor Titus yeldho
Patriarchal Vicar

Foreword

In the Book of Ecclesiastes, King Solomon said, "Of making many books there is no end, and much study is wearisome to the flesh" (Ecclesiastes 12:12). There are so many books written on the Person of Christ and the Faith of the Church. However, not all books are the same. Some stand out as having made a difference, not as "wearisome to the flesh" but as lifting the spirit of the faith to heights of greater knowledge, wisdom and truth regarding what we profess. Father Joseph's book, We Believe in One True God, is an exposition of the Christology of the Syrian Orthodox Church. This book is an apologetic attempt among the Western theological scholarship to ascertain that the Christology of the Syrian Orthodox Church is one and the same of the undivided Early Church. Father Joseph took great pain to find the influence of the Christology of Cyril of Alexandria on the Christology of the Syrian Orthodox Church. The exposition of the Christology of the Church is made through stages by stage in the Eucharistic Liturgy and the liturgical development over the centuries.

Bishop's House, New Jersey
March 31, 2023

+ Titus Yeldho, archbishop

MALANKARA ARCHDIOCESE
of the Syrian Orthodox Church in North America
(Under the Holy Apostolic Throne of Antioch and All the East)

Archbishop Mor Titus yeldho
Patriarchal Vicar

The theme of the book is very much on the task to establish that the Faith of the Church is in its Prayer. This is a book to be read not only by Theologians but also by everyone who is seeking the answers to the most important questions about the Person of Christ and what we believe. This book is the first work of Father Joseph and is mostly based on his research for his master's degree. As the apostle Peter stated that God's "divine power has given to us all things that pertain to life and godliness, through the knowledge of Him who called us by glory and virtue" (2 Peter 1:3). This work is reminding once again to steadfast in God's Word and adhere to the teachings of the Fathers of the Church and its Holy Tradition. This book is a reminder for all of us that faith should be based on the Scripture and the Tradition, because "faith comes by hearing, and hearing by the word of God" (Romans 10:17). My prayer and hope are that much fruit will be harvested for the kingdom of Christ and the glory of the Holy Church through this book and through future endeavors. I wish Father Joseph with great success and blessings on his continued work on the Christology of the Syrian Orthodox Church. May God Bless him abundantly.

Bishop's House, New Jersey
March 31, 2023

+ Titus Yeldho, archbishop

TABLE OF CONTENTS

Introduction 1

Chapter 1: A Christological Problem. 5

Chapter 2: Historical Development of the Liturgy of the Syrian Orthodox Church 21

Chapter 3: The Jewish background of the Christian Faith 34

Chapter 4: Education Through Liturgy 49

Chapter 5: Lex Orandi, Lex Credendi 57

Chapter 6: The Christological Development through the Centuries. 73

Chapter 7: Development of the Liturgy under the Church Fathers 90

Chapter 8: Christology in the Prayers and Liturgies of the Syrian Orthodox Church 107

- Chapter. 9: Christology Today: 170
- Chapter 10: General Conclusion: 179
- The Final Point. 182
- Bibliography 185

Introduction

In the history of salvation, the liturgy of the Church, both East and West, has played the role of providing a common heritage of worship among God's people. Most liturgies have developed over time and have adapted to new environments to reflect the evolution of culture. The liturgy is the prayer of the Church, guided by the Holy Spirit and in which Christ becomes contemporary and enters int our lives (Ratzinger 2000:7). The liturgy of the Syriac Orthodox Church is no exception, as the Christological differences that arose at the Council of Chalcedon emboldened the Syriac Orthodox Church to emphasize its position in its Eucharistic liturgy. In particular, the Fraction Rite in the Syriac Orthodox Church's liturgy was more strongly emphasized; thus, we can view it as an explanation of the Syrian Orthodox Church's understanding of, and faith in, the full divinity and humanity of Christ. The main focus of this paper concerns how the faith of the Syriac Orthodox Church is expressed through its liturgical practices, especially in the Fraction Rite. In many ways, the Fraction Rite is a microcosm of the Christological position of the Syrian Orthodox Church. In particular, the significance of breaking of the sacramental bread into particles and the co-mingling, the use of leavened bread (which is peculiar to the Orthodox churches in general), the hymns which accompany these actions, and even the positions of the sacramental bread on the paten, are all ways in which the Syrian Eucharistic liturgy bespeaks that community's faith in the personhood of Christ. This thesis endeavors to analyze these various aspects of the Fraction Rite in order to come to a deeper understanding of the Syriac Orthodox Church's Christological position.

The Church of Antioch was a very prominent among all churches and vastly spread to the Middle East, China and India. By the second century itself, Bible was translated into Aramaic and is known as Peshitta and widely used by the Syrian Christian communities in and around the Middle East, Mesopotamia and India. The language, culture and history of the Syrian Church and its people were known through the writings by Church Fathers like Michael Rabo (10th century) and Ignatius Barsoum (20thth century). These writings complemented with the literary histories and bibliographies Assemani, Wright, Duval, Chabot and Baumstark as well as collections of European and Syrian manuscripts helped modern scholarship known about the history, language, christology and practices of the Syrian Orthodox Church. The scholarly audio, video and written work of Sebastian Brock on "the Syriac

Orthodox Church and its Ancient Aramaic Heritage" (The Hidden Pearl 2001) is a contemporary scholarly work on the Syrian orthodox Church.

The Syrian Orthodox Church recognizes only the first three Ecumenical Councils- the first Council of Nicaea, the first Council of Constantinople and the first Council of Ephesus. Church rejected the definitions of the Council of Chalcedon held in AD 451 in the Roman city of Chalcedon. Church also rejected the teachings of both Nestorius and Eutyches as well. In the Council of Chalcedon (c. 451), the Syrian Orthodox Church along with the Coptic Orthodox Church, both then are known as Alexandrines, separated from the Byzantine and Roman Christians rejected the definitions of union of two natures of Christ. The teachings and its doctrine of the Syrian Orthodox Church clearly believed in God incarnate, with His divinity and humanity fully present and united without mixture, confusion or change. As concerning two natures of Christ, the Church unwaveringly upheld the formula of St. Cyril of Alexandria which was accepted by both Chalcedonian and non-Chalcedonian Churches equally. The Church kept St. Cyril's formula of "One nature of God the Logos incarnates which reveals the Hypostatic union of natures, the divine and the human in one without mingling, nor confusion, nor alteration." Even though the non-Chalcedonian Churches are wrongly accused with the Eutychianism, the Church has vehemently denied it since the very beginning and affirmably withstand with two natures of the Word incarnate.

Chapter 1: A Christological Problem.

Whenever I meet the western protestant theologians and introduce myself as a Syrian Christian, interestingly enough, people mentioned me as "oh you are from one of those monophysite churches". Some people even looking at me as I am something like an "exotic" Christian still follow the "heretic" theology of "Jesus has only one nature". I did ask myself time to time "Am I a heretic"? As I read the western and eastern orthodox theologians' writings about the Syrian Orthodox Church and I see nothing else other than "it is heretic".

Even though, the Non-Chalcedon churches, which include the Syrian Orthodox Church, rejected and condemned the teachings of Eutyches (that Christ has but one nature after the incarnation), some Christians, still treated the Non-Chalcedon as Eutychians or Monophysites. The fundamental problem here is the failure of the western theologians to do deep research on the doctrines professed by the non-Chalcedon churches. My quest to learn about the doctrinal stand of my own faith revealed to me that doctrine is that matters and heresy is the opposite and dangerous to understand the knowledge about who Jesus is. The Syrian orthodox Church, like all other churches claim that the revelation of God, through Jesus Christ, is definitive and complete (Heb 1:2). So, Jesus is the central piece of any research and true knowledge about him is an essential part of our faith.

The fundamental research problem in my research is whether the faith of the Syrian Orthodox Church is Orthodoxy or Heterodoxy. This question is explored historically, doctrinally and biblically. The teachings of Cyril of Alexandria on the Hypostatic Union of two natures of Christ will be explored and explained with the teachings of the Syrian Orthodox Church fathers such as Severus Antioch. Special attention will be given how polarized the early Church into two camps after the second and third Ecumenical Councils in Constantinople and in Ephesus. The influence of Nestorius and Eutychus teachings under the ecclesiastical, political and regional turf in the Roman Emperor and the failures to unify the Universal Church at the Ecumenical Council of Chalcedon.

Who We Are?

The history of the Syrian Orthodox Church and the establishment of its Patriarchate goes back to A.D. 37. In the Acts 11:26 recounts "it was in Antioch that the disciples were fist called

Christians". The Patristic history of the Syrian Orthodox Church can trace back to the early Christianity in Antioch. The church historian Eusebius, in his *Chronicon* (1,2) tells us that Peter the Apostle established a bishopric in Antioch and became its first bishop. Eusebius also tells us that Peter was succeeded by Evodius. In the work of *Historia Ecclesiastica*, Eusebius again told us that Ignatius, the illuminator was the second after Peter in the bishopric of Antioch (Syriac Orthodox Resources). In the middle of the fifth century, the bishops of Antioch, Alexandria, Byzantium and Rome were called the patriarchs. The bishop of Antioch accepted the title name of Ignatius, after the illuminator and the see of Antioch continually flourished till today and Ignatius Ephrem II is the 123rd bishop of Antioch today as the head of the Syrian Orthodox Church of Antioch.

The Church of Antioch was a very prominent among all churches and vastly spread to the Middle East, China and India. By the second century itself, Bible was translated into Aramaic and is known as Peshitta and widely used by the Syrian Christian communities in and around the Middle East, Mesopotamia and India. The language, culture and history of the Syrian Church and its people were known through the writings by Church Fathers like Michael Rabo (10th century) and Ignatius Barsoum

(20th century). These writings complemented with the literary histories and bibliographies Assemani, Wright, Duval, Chabot and Baumstark as well as collections of European and Syrian manuscripts helped modern scholarship known about the history, language, Christology and practices of the Syrian Orthodox Church. The scholarly audio, video and written work of Sebastian Brock on "the Syriac Orthodox Church and its Ancient Aramaic Heritage" (The Hidden Pearl 2001) is a contemporary scholarly work on the Syrian orthodox Church.

The term 'Monophysites' used to call the non-chalcedonian churches is "comparatively a modern term" (Samuel 2001:22f). The Western theologians thought that using "Monophysites" is of convenience and sufficient enough because the non-Caledonian churches adhere to "one incarnate nature". The "Eutychianism" or "Monophysitism" is a distorted version of the Christology of the Syrian Orthodox Church. According to Samuel "the term 'one' in the 'one incarnate nature of God the Word' cannot legitimately be rendered as the *monos* of the *Monophysites"* (Samuel 2001: 243). The Church as always maintained, from the 6th century to today, not to use the phrase "one nature" in reference to Christ without the phrase "incarnate". So the "one" in the phrase is not a simple one but it is a composite nature of Godhead and manhood as asserted in the Christology of the Syrian Orthodox Church.

Heinrich Fries and Karl Rahner wrote that the fundamental obligation of the Church is to unite in Jesus Christ and in one another as expressed in the Holy Scripture, in the Apostolic teachings, and in the Nicene-Constantinople Creed (1983:7). The biggest scandal of the Church today is the division and excommunication of churches amongst themselves. The first division following the Nicene-Constantinople councils happened at the General Council of Chalcedon in AD 451 where the Antiochene Church strongly reacted against the Alexandrian Church by declaring that Christ is one person but two natures (Ware 1963:34). The Syrian Orthodox Church, along with the Alexandrian Church, rejected the Council of Chalcedon on the ground that it defined the two natures of Christ in an "adoption of Nestorian formula of Christ in two natures" (Ishak 2013:553). The doctrinal position of the Syrian Orthodox Church was "One Nature of Christ" as the composite Christ is one nature and one *qnumo* (hypostasis) (Rabo 2014:271). Because of this position, the Syrian Orthodox Church was wrongly labelled "Monophysite" (Ware 1963:33). The Syrian Church had a most celebrated school in Edessa and St. Ephraim and other most venerated Fathers of the Church are the products of this school. Unfortunately, the early history of the Syrian Orthodox Church was suppressed by then Emperor Zeno, in AD 489 (Etheridge 2018:118).

Most of the Eastern Orthodox churches claimed the Alexandrian and the Syrian Orthodox churches were followers of Eutychianism which argues that before the incarnation of Christ, the Godhead and manhood "were united in Jesus Christ, He was of two natures," but Christ became "one nature" after the incarnation (Samuel 2001:39). Even though the non-Chalcedonian churches and the Syrian Orthodox church condemned this position throughout the history of the Church (Samuel 2001:40), the Chalcedonian churches called the non-Chalcedonian churches heterodox because they profess "one incarnate nature" in which Christ's human nature is lost, arguing Christ was one *ousia* (Samuel 1987:119). The misunderstanding of the position of Christ having "two natures" before the union goes back to the sixth century when the Antiochian theologian John the Grammarian criticized his opponent, Severus of Antioch, accusing him of believing that "the Godhead and the flesh of Christ constituted one *ousia* and one nature" (Samuel 2001:42). The Christological disputes were extended because of the language barriers of the non-Greek-speaking Alexandrian churches who failed to grasp the full extent of the Greek terms in their own languages and cultures (Florovsky 1987:47).

The anathema against the Syrian Church Fathers such as Severus and Dioscorus is still standing and cannot be revoked as it is imposed and affirmed by 4th, 5th and 6th Ecumenical Councils (Toroczkai 2016:257). The Eastern Orthodox Churches accepted seven ecumenical councils, while the Alexandrian Church, now known as the Oriental Orthodox Churches (Coptic, Syrian, Armenian, Ethiopian, Eritrean and Indian) only accept the first three as ecumenical councils. Even though there were efforts made in last 1400 years to reconcile between Chalcedon and non-Chalcedon churches, these anathemas have been major roadblocks to reconciliation.

Unlike the Western perception of the Christological triumph of the Ecumenical Council at Chalcedon (A.D. 451), Kurt Aland (1985) viewed it as a complete failure and a division which lasted into the present era. At the Council of Chalcedon, they agreed on the unity of God and man but failed to explain how. The fifth-century church generally accepted that "Christ was truly God and truly man," but they differed in defining "what truly human" meant concerning Christ (McGukin 2004:136). The Alexandrian Church accepted the Cyrillian Christological union, *henosis ek dyo physeon* (union from out of two natures), but the Antiochians went along with the formula of Nestorius that *en dyo physesin* (Christ in two natures) (McGukin 2004:136-137). Instead of resolving the issue of the unity of Christ, the division and controversy began and continued in full force. The lack of will to listen to opposing views and the political muscle exerted by the Roman Empire resulted in favoritism towards the Chalcedonian supporters. The non-Chalcedonian patriarchs and bishops were persecuted, excommunicated, and banished into exile. The formula of unity did not bring any fruit as both factions lost trust in each other, and the Roman Empire lost its political will to find an enduring solution. This ultimately resulted in a larger, permanent schism that continues to the present time.

The Syrian Orthodox Church, along with the other non-Chalcedonian churches, confirmed, believed, and taught that at the Incarnation, the Son of God united Himself to manhood, animated with a rational soul and of the same substance with us, that He suffered in His passions in reality in body and soul, and that there was no confusion or mixture of the natures in Him (Samuel 1964:46). The Fathers of churches who opposed at the Council of Chalcedon, including the Syrian Orthodox Church, was led to oppose not because of their sympathy towards Eutychus's teachings or alignment with Monophysite teachings, as alleged, but because of their real understanding of the term "one incarnate nature of God the Word" (Samuel 1964:46). In his third letter to Nestorius, St. Cyril of Alexandria explained that the hypostatic union was a "natural union," a radical and concrete union that the soul of man has with its own body (McGuckin 1994:212.) At the Council of Chalcedon, Cyril's "Miaphysite" theology was accepted (Weinandy 2003:47).

The Christology of the non-Chalcedonian Churches, including the Syrian Orthodox Church, formally consolidated based on the *mia physis* Christology under Severus of Antioch in the sixth century (Behr 1998:23). It was Severus who was instrumental in defining Cyril of Alexandria's *mia physis* into a philosophical context and providing the Christological standard for the non-Chalcedonian churches (Behr 1998:24). Severus argues that one hypostatic union from two natures involves one *prosopon* and one nature incarnate of God the Word. Severus clarified this term and said the "one" in the "one incarnate nature of God the Word" cannot legitimately be rendered as the *monos* of the "Monophysites" (Samuel 2001:243). For Severus, the union of two natures in Christ is "composite" in nature (Behr 1998:29-30), where the individual *prosopon* remain undiminished and real, but they only exist in one unity (Behr 1998: 30). For Severus, the hypostasis of Christ is the composite hypostasis "formed from the union between God and man in the incarnation" (Behr 1998:32). The festal letters and homilies of Severus are the doctrinal stamp of the Syrian Orthodox Church.

The Eastern Orthodox theologian Meyendorff explained the term "Miaphysite" as *mia,* meaning "one" but "not single one" or "simple numerical one" (Meyendorff 2011:17). As such, St. Cyril's hypostatic union of the natures of Christ does not "consist of a simple cooperation" but of a union of divine and human natures without any duplication of the personality of the "one incarnated God and man" (Meyendorff 2011:17). A discussion on the Christology of Philoxenos of Mabbug (d.523) by Michelson (2014) is noticeably strong in the Miaphysite defence against the Chalcedonian Christology. The inherent problem of understanding the Miaphysite Christology was that many scholars of the West were either ignorant of or have been negligent towards the study of Miaphysite Christology in detail, thus relegating the anti-Chalcedonian Church as something "exotic" in the greater Christian landscape (Michelson 2014:7).

In the later part of the sixth century and early seventh century, the Chalcedonian theologians coined the new term "monophysite." This was a term used for the sake of convenience (Frend 1972:22) to refer to those who rejected the Council of Chalcedon and the Tome of Leo because of the insistence on using the term "in two natures." The "monophysite" terminology implied "one nature" instead of "one composite nature," and the non-Chalcedonian churches have been branded as "monophysite" in much of church history (Samuel 2001:236). Despite all this, neither Cyril of Alexandria nor Pope Dioscorus of Alexandria, who chaired the second Council of Ephesus, accepted at any time the notion of "Eutychianism" or "Monophysitism" (Samuel 2001:293).

To attempt to clarify their position and avoid any confusion or misunderstanding of their preferred expression of "one composite nature," the Oriental Orthodox Church began to use the term *mia physis* to refer to "one composite nature" (Aydin 2016:288). Through this clarification, a fresh initiative began for the opposing sides to understand each other's position on the key terms such as *physis* and *hypostasis* (Aydin 2016:291). Instead of forcing uniformity of terminology, a unity of faith based on the formulation of the doctrinal formula of the Council of Chalcedon was the goal, even in recent ecumenical dialogues between the Eastern Orthodox and the Oriental Orthodox Churches (Aydin 2016:292). In one of the dialogues between the Eastern Orthodox and the Oriental Orthodox Churches, Father V.C. Samuel (1998) simply stated that, for the Syrian Orthodox Church, Christ does not exist "in two natures," the two natures exist in Him, each in its own perfection and reality (Aydin 2016: 298).

Thorough further theological dialogue and an ongoing, determined interaction between the Catholic and the Syrian Orthodox Churches, they finally came to terms with their Christological differences. The Syrian Orthodox Church's Christological position was more or less agreed to by the Catholic Church as both Prelates, Pope John Paul II and Patriarch Ignatius Zakka I, signed a common declaration of faith in 1984 in which they jointly declared that Jesus is "perfect God as to His divinity and perfect man as to His humanity." They both affirmed that the "divinity is united to His humanity" and that the "union is real, perfect, without blending or mingling, without confusion, without alteration, without division, without the least separation" (Aydin 2016:299).

At the World Council of Churches' General Assembly held in Nairobi, Kenya in 1975, which called for a "Conciliar Fellowship" among her members, a new level of reconciliation and acceptance was evident among the non-Chalcedonian and Chalcedonian Churches. This paved the way for "Conciliar Fellowship" and resulted in the issuing of the first unofficial, agreed statement of reconciliation between the two church bodies (Chalcedon and non-Chalcedon) in which the "theology of St. Cyril of Alexandria" was used (Gregorios 1981:11) as a starting point. In the second agreed statement, both families affirm that "the Hypostasis of Logos became composite, by uniting to His divine nature, with its natural will and energy" (Behr 1998:28), united hypostatically. This was also an acceptance of the Christology of St. Severus whom the Chalcedonian Churches decried as a heretic.

In the Unofficial Consultation between theologians of Eastern Orthodox and Oriental Orthodox Churches, which began in 1964 in Aarhus and continued in three subsequent meetings (Bristol 1967, Geneva 1970 and Addis Ababa 1971), the two sides came to an agreement that the Oriental Orthodox Churches agreed with the Byzantine Orthodox Churches and condemned the teachings of both Eutychus and Nestorius (Gregorios 2016). The first official joint sub commission of Oriental and Eastern Orthodox Churches released an official statement in September 1987 summarizing that "Jesus Christ, the Incarnate Word of God unites in his hypostasis the nature of God and the nature of humanity in one single hypostasis and one united divine-human nature, though the Byzantine prefer to say two natures inseparably united" (Gregorios 2016). This agreement affirms that the Christology of the Syrian Orthodox Church and the Oriental Orthodox Churches, in general, are in conformity with the Eastern Orthodox, Catholic and Protestant Churches. The Christology of the Syrian Orthodox

Church is in line with the rest of the Christendom, and there is no reason to call the non-Chalcedonian Churches, including the Syrian Orthodox Church, heretics. The division is not essentially doctrinal but rather a Hellenistic cultural imposition by the Greek Church on the Africans and Asians, much like Western churches today who try to impose terminology and frameworks of theology on the Oriental Orthodox Churches (Gregorios 1964).

The Oriental Orthodox Churches have been in consultation with various individual Protestant Churches on Christological topics and on September 13, 1994 they signed an "Agreed Statement of Christology" with Reformed Churches in the Netherlands (www.ukmidcopts.org). On November 19, 2002, the Anglican-Oriental Orthodox International Commission signed an "Agreed Statement on Christology" as well (www.anglicancommunion.org).

The Syrian Orthodox Church recently declared the acceptance of the general statements of faith between the Eastern and Oriental Orthodox Churches as well as the Common declaration on the faith by the Syrian Orthodox Church and the Catholic Church (Aydin 2016:288). This is a great beginning and assurance toward healing the Christological differences through dialogue.

Even though these theological consultations are happening among the Church bodies, there is a strong refusal for a meaningful dialogue from the Eastern Orthodox theologians. In an Inter-Orthodox Theological Conference on Ecumenism sponsored by the School of Pastoral Theology at the Aristotelian University in Thessaloniki in September 2004, they declared that "Dialogues with the Monophysites are total fruitlessness and compromise on matters of faith" (Seraphim 2005). The Conference declared that "Statements issued at the theological consultations between eastern and oriental churches" were unacceptable (Seraphim 2005). A large number of Eastern orthodox clerics, monastics and even the laymen expect acceptance of their Christology and terminology of the "key dogmatic position" as they think anything other than theirs is heretical (Asproulis 2016:259).

There is a gap of understanding of the Christology of the Syrian Orthodox Church among the modern scholars of Christology. I intend to fill this gap by connecting the Christology of Cyril of Alexandria and Severus of Antioch to the Christology of the Syrian Orthodox Church. In the current theological scholarship, the Christological position of the Syrian Orthodox Church is either misread or not fully comprehended, and my work intends to fill that vacuum and serve as a platform for further theological discussion. Since the Eastern and the Syrian orthodox churches consider their Christology as rooted in the teachings of the Cyril of Alexandria (Seraphim 2005), my work will answer the question of how the *mia physis* Christology of Cyril of Alexandria help shaped the Christology of the Syrian Orthodox Church and how the Christology of the Syrian Orthodox Church is one and the same of the undivided Church. It will show that the Syrian Orthodox Church is not a Monophysite Church. Father John Romanides of the Eastern Orthodox church correctly said that "perhaps Leo of Rome and Dioscorus of Alexandria both are orthodox because they both accepted the Christology of Cyril" (Romanides 1994) who had a Christology which "encompasses the whole faith of the one undivided church of the early centuries" (Bishoy 1989).

Chapter 2: Historical Development of the Liturgy of the Syrian Orthodox Church

Our Lord instituted the Eucharist on the night of his Passion and commanded his disciples to commemorate this mystery until his Second Coming. Based on the traditions and teachings of the Fathers of the Church, it is often held that the first to celebrate the Eucharist was St. James, the brother of our Lord, who received this tradition orally from Christ. The Syrian Orthodox Church historian Archbishop Ishaq Saka describes how the tradition of Eucharist was handed over:

> After receiving the Holy Spirit in the upper room on Sunday, they, on the next day, consecrated the Sacrament of the Chrism, and on the third day offered the divine oblation. The first to perform this service was St. James, brother of the Lord, who received [it] orally from the Lord himself. He handed it over to John, the beloved disciple, who celebrated the sacrifice on Wednesday. The Mother of God partook in this

communion after she was baptized. All of this was done in the upper room according to the church's tradition.[1]

According to Paul Bradshaw, "because the narratives were passed on within Christian communities which celebrated the Eucharist,"[2] we can assert with some confidence that John conveyed the instructions for the liturgy to his disciples and then to their disciples and to the early Christian communities. According to the "teachings of the Syriac Orthodox Church,"[3] these instructions were originally handed down in the Aramaic language, and the Syriac Orthodox Church has continued to follow these instructions faithfully, also safeguarding the Aramaic dialect through the liturgy.

The very foundation of the early liturgy originated in Jewish religious practices, as the early Apostolic Church preserved and maintained many of the liturgical forms in Jewish worship. In reconstructing

---

[1] Ishaq Saka, *Commentary on the Liturgy of the Syrian Orthodox Church of Antioch,* trans. Matti Moosa (Piscataway, NJ: Gorgias Press, 2008), 13.

[2] Paul Bradshaw, *Search for the Origins of Christian Worship* (London: Oxford University Press, 2002), 62-63.

[3] Titus Yeldho, *A Guide to the Holy Qurbono* (Whippany, NJ: MSOSSA, 2012), 56.

the Jewish background to Christian worship, Paul Bradshaw notes that

> [i]n our efforts to assess the influence of Jewish practices upon Christian worship we ought to focus primarily upon the first century. It is true that contact between Jews and Christians did not end after 70 AD, and there is evidence for some continuing links down to at least the fourth century; some of the early Fathers were clearly influenced by Jewish sources, and John Chrysostom tells us that some ordinary Christians were attending both synagogue and church, though it is not clear how widespread, geographically or chronologically, this practice was.[4]

The tradition of the Church and the Scriptures teach how the Eucharist began in the upper room at the Last Supper, as recounted in all four Gospels (see Matt 26:17–30; Mark 14:12–26; Luke 22:7–23; and John 13:1–20) and how the early Church obeyed Jesus's command to "break bread" in his name (Acts 2:42). But how was this memorial meal transformed into the highly ritualistic Eucharistic service it is

---

[4] Bradshaw, *Search for the Origins of Christian Worship,* 33.

today? Josef Jungmann suggests a theory of the development of the Eucharist in the first century:

"The Apostles fulfilled the command of our Lord given them at the Last Supper by celebrating regularly in the setting of a meal which was conducted with the ritual forms of Jewish community meal."[5] The supper meal included blessings over the bread and wine, the breaking of the bread, and *koinonia,* a Greek word which first occurs in Acts 2:42 and which means "fellowship, sharing in common, communion." The basic structure of the first part of the liturgy was apparently adapted from the Jewish evening service for the Sabbath that was celebrated at the time of our Lord. The essential elements included an opening greeting, followed by a lesson from the Scripture. Immediately after that followed the psalmody and a lesson. The sermon was next, and then followed the dismissal of the non-baptized, consisting of prayers and dismissal. The earliest evidence of such a structure is from the *First Apology* of Justin Martyr, as summarized by Paul Bradshaw in the following passage:

---

[5] Josef Jungmann, *The Mass of the Roman Rite: Its Origins and Development*, trans. Francis Brunner (Note Dame, IN: Ave Maria Press, 2012), 9.

Justin Martyr writing at Rome in the middle of the second century, merely says that "the records of the apostles or the writings of the prophets are read for as long as time allows. Then, when the reader has finished, the president in a discourse admonishes and exhorts [us] to imitate these good things. Then we will stand up together and offer prayers"[6]

Many scholars thus indicate that the first part of the liturgy was developed, more or less, from the Jewish meal service. Because of the steady growth of the community, these table prayers were transformed into a larger communal setting as Jungmann explains:

> The growing communities became too large for these domestic table-gatherings… Tables disappeared from the room, except for the one at which the presiding official pronounced the Eucharist over the bread and wine. The room was broadened into a large hall capable of holding the whole congregation. Only in isolated instances was

---

[6] Bradshaw, *Search for the Origins of Christian Worship,* 123.

the connection with the meal continued into the following centuries.[7]

By the second century, primitive expressions like "breaking the bread" and "Lord's Supper" were replaced by the term "Eucharist," as seen in the writings of Ignatius of Antioch (107AD)[8] and Justin Martyr (165AD).[9] There were few innovations in the celebration of the liturgy such as "inclusion of gifts brought by the faithful" and adding "milk and honey" for the newly baptized. However, more or less, the structure of the liturgy remained the same.

Evidence from early manuscripts reveals that an apostolic stamp of approval was normally given to matters of liturgical practices and orders. For example, the publication of the *Didache* (the Teaching of the Twelve Apostles) in 1883 after a rediscovery of the Greek manuscripts, offered insight into the early Eucharistic celebration, which has all the hallmarks of the two-part event we know

---

[7] Jungmann, *Mass of the Roman Rite*, 10.

[8] Ignatius of Antioch, *Letter to the Smyrnaeans*, trans. Cyril C. Richardson. Early Christian Fathers (Grand Rapids, MI: Christian Classical Ethereal Library, 1953), 95.

[9] Justin the Martyr, The *First Apology*, trans. Cyril C. Richardson. Early Christian Fathers (Grand Rapids, MI: Christian Classical Ethereal Library, 1953), 222.

today: the liturgy for the catechumens and the liturgy for the baptized.

The *Apostolic Constitutions* (a collection of eight treatises alleged to be the work of the twelve Apostles written c.375–380 AD) is an additional major source of the Syriac Orthodox Church's liturgical history. Book Two provides an outline of the *Anaphora,* and a full Anaphora is contained in Book Seven. Early Church Fathers, such as John of Damascus of Syria (675-749 AD), accepted the *Apostolic Constitutions* as canonical.

The early Syriac work *Didascalia Apostolorum,*[10] which was translated by Paul de Lagarde in 1854, also provides important information about liturgical practices in the ancient Church of Antioch. The *Didascalia Apostolorum*, a treatise written in the early third century, contains what is described as the teachings of the twelve Apostles, which as we have already noted, was a claim common among church orders. According to F. L. Cross and E. L Livingstone, the *Apostolic Church Order* was another "early Christian document containing regulations on ecclesiastical practice and moral discipline. Its contents are ascribed to various

---

[10] R. Hugh Connolly, *Didascalia Apostolorum* (Toronto, Cross Reach Publications, 2017), 31, Kindle.

Apostles."[11] The Syriac liturgy is more or less also indebted to John Chrysostom (347–407AD), who gave extensive homilies on the liturgical practices of the early Church. Another ancient source that reveals the liturgical practices of the Syriac liturgy is the homilies of "Theodore of Mopsuestia (350–428AD)."[12]

Since its beginnings, the Syriac Orthodox Church has celebrated the liturgy of St. James in Aramaic. The 32nd canon of the Trullanic Synod that met in Constantinople in 693AD, and which criticized the Armenians for their lack of a mixed chalice, referred to Saint James as its authority:

> For also James, the brother, according to the flesh of Christ our God, to whom the throne of the Church of the Jerusalem first was entrusted, and Basil, the Archbishop of the Church of Caesarea, whose glory has spread through all the world, when they delivered to us directions for the mystical sacrifice in writing, declared that the holy chalice is

---

[11] F. L. Cross and E. L. Livingstone, eds., "Apostolic Church Order" in *The Oxford Dictionary of the Christian Church*, 3rd rev. ed. (Oxford: Oxford University Press, 2005), 32.

[12] Bradshaw, *Origins of Christian Worship*, 109.

consecrated in the divine Liturgy with water and wine.[13]

The Liturgy of St. James, which was originally celebrated in the church of Jerusalem, slowly found its way to the Syrian and Greek provinces. Father Louis Duchesne (1843-1922AD), an eminent philologist, says, "The fact that the Jacobites have preserved the James liturgy in Syriac as their fundamental liturgy proves that it was already consecrated by long use at the time when these communities took their rise—that is to say, about the middle of the sixth century."[14] The Liturgy of St. James grew into two distinctive liturgical traditions: the Greek tradition of St. James and the Syriac tradition of St. James, which have been followed by the Chalcedonians and non-Chalcedonians, respectively.

As will be noted throughout this study, the liturgical prayers and anthems of the Syriac Orthodox Church express the Church's faith and

---

[13] Council in Trullo, Canon 33, last modified 2009, accessed March 10, 2017, http://www.newadvent.org/fathers/3814.htm.

[14] Louis Duchesne, *Christian Worship, Its Origin and Evolution: A Study of the Latin Liturgy up to the Time of Charlemagne* (London: Society for Promoting Christian Knowledge, 1910), 54.

Christology.[15] For example, the language and prayers concerning the Eucharist that developed over the years conceptualize the idea of the divine Lord Incarnate as "begotten without beginning, beyond times and origins who came down from heaven." The prayers are addressed to the Father, the First Person in the Trinity, because the celebrant, the Priest, is representing Christ in the Eucharist; as such, he is a mediator between God the Father and the faithful. Strictly speaking, the exchange of predicates between the divine and human natures of Christ in the Eucharist is not often used except in a few places where the Incarnation is highlighted. The series of petitions that begin, "who by his birth, etc." and "to whom immortality belongs naturally," addresses the "merciful God" without any change of subjects or any distinctions of divine and human nature of God. But this is not the case in the Epiphany prayer, which says, "by your body and blood we have gained life. O Good One who fashioned us from the dust…." Here, the subject of address is directly the Second Person of the Trinity—in this case, the Word made flesh who

---

[15] For example, the various litanies and petitions in the Syriac Orthodox Church's Eucharistic liturgy end with "who" or "to whom" they are addressed: *e.g.*, "O merciful God who in mercy governs all, we beseech you." These prayers do not make any distinction between the divine and human attributes of God Incarnate.

gives us his own sanctifying Body and Blood, not the other way around.

By the twelfth century, new elements had been added to the liturgy, including a Fraction Rite (the focus of this thesis) through which the Church asserted her Christology. Father Baby Varghese, a professor in the Malankara Orthodox Church in India, has explained the timing of the additions made in the Syriac Orthodox liturgy. According to Varghese, "New elements were introduced, such as elaborate preparation rites, dramatic blessing of the censer in the pre-anaphora, inaudible prayers and an elaborate fraction."[16] Varghese dates the elaboration of the fraction to the ninth and tenth centuries with the addition of a series of complex rites and prayers articulating the mystery of the Passion, noting that as late as the eleventh century, some dioceses were still using a simple fraction. However, by the twelfth century, the latter had been replaced with a longer formula in which the various gestures of the fraction are related to the Passion, Death, and Resurrection of Christ.

---

[16] Baby Varghese, *West Syrian Liturgical Theology,* Liturgy, Worship and Society Series (Ashgate, Aldershot, England: 2004), 13.

In conclusion, the history of the liturgy of the Syrian Orthodox Church coincides with the development of Christianity in its expansion and growth throughout the world. The roots of its liturgy may be traced back to the Upper Room on the day of the Last Supper. On the day of the Last Supper, Jesus gathered his twelve disciples not only to commemorate the Passover but also to establish a new covenant with his Body and Blood. After the Resurrection, the new community gathered around the Body and Blood of Christ to commemorate the covenant established by Jesus. The new Church adapted and followed the Jewish table meal services with bread and wine on the Lord's Day instead of the Sabbath. Subsequently, the table services gave way to larger community gatherings. The language and the practices of Eucharist said to have been conducted by none other than St. James, the brother of our Lord, were faithfully observed by the Syriac Orthodox Church throughout the centuries. During the Christological controversies, the Church began to assert its belief through its liturgical practices, including the Fraction Rite. As will be noted in detail in the subsequent chapters, the most distinctive contribution of the Syriac Orthodox Church to Christological doctrine is its insistence on the oneness of the Person of Christ, which was explained as resulting from the real union of his divinity and humanity. Within the changed ecclesial, cultural, and geographical context of the fourth and fifth centuries, the Eucharistic liturgy of the Syrian Orthodox Church began to assume a shape and content that are distinctive to the faith of that Church.

Chapter 3: The Jewish background of the Christian Faith

The twenty first century Church is in the midst of an identity crisis. The problem is that they worship a Jesus whom they don't know fully who he is. Christians are not probably fully aware of their roots and may think and believe that the Christian history began with Jesus Christ 2000 years back. It is true that with Jesus, a new covenant was established which guaranteed forgiveness of sins and the eternal life for those who believed in him. In the Old Testament, God has also made covenant with Father Abraham and promised him that his descendants will be heirs of the Kingdom of Heaven. According to Apostle Paul " For Christ is the end of the law for righteousness to everyone who believes." (Romans 10:4) Through Christ we become joint heirs to all the promises God gave to Abraham, in whom our spiritual roots are founded. It was God's sovereign choice to choose Abraham and his descendants to be the lineage through which Messiah would ultimately have to come.

Who is Jesus?

Jesus was born to Jewish parents, raised as an observant Jew, follows the law and traditions, and lived in his entire life within the context of Jewish community. He never intended to abolish the Law, and made that clear in Gospel of Matthew 5:17, "Do not think that I have come to abolish the Law or the Prophets; I have not come to abolish them but to fulfill them."

Dr. Marvin Wilson, a Professor of Biblical and Theological studies at Gordon College and a leading scholar on Christian-Jewish relations writes, "Jesus was a Jew, not a Christian of Gentile origin. His teachings, like those of his followers, reflect a distinct ethnicity and culture. The evidence found in the New Testament is abundantly clear: as mother gives birth and nourishes a child, so Hebrew culture and language gave birth to and nourishes Christianity."[17] In the genealogy of Jesus in the Gospels of Mathew and Luke, the writers clearly identified Jesus as the offspring of Abraham through the royal line of David. The genealogical records again help us to go back to the roots of Jesus and his

---

[17] Wilson, Marvin, *Our Father Abraham: Jewish roots of the Christian Faith* (Wm B. Eerdmans Publishing Company, Grand Rapids, Michigan) p.12.

Jewish origin. For the Jews, genealogy is very important as the ancestry (1) determined one's claim on land, and (2) claims on rights of inheritance, royalty, priesthood and for Jesus, proof of his Messianic claim and right to the Davidic throne.

The Church:

Saint Paul described in his epistle to Romans 11:24 that the Church is a branch from a wild Olive tree, which is Israel, and has firmly rooted in a rich Hebraic soil first established through the Old Testament patriarch Abraham. The Church is an offspring from that wild Olive tree which is Father Abraham as said by Paul again in Romans 4:16. "Therefore, the promise comes by faith, so that it may be by grace and may be guaranteed to all Abraham's offspring—not only to those who are of the law but also to those who have the faith of Abraham. He is the father of us all." (Romans 4:16) There is no evidence in the Gospels that Jesus ever promoted a church that is separated from the God's chosen people, Israel. On the contrary, the New Testament established that the believing gentiles as Abraham's spiritual sons and daughters who then become entitled to the full covenant blessings as well. Because of this adoption (Romans 4:16) the history of Israel and the Jewish people has become the foundational family history of the Church as well. Saint Paul is very clear about this when he said; "The mystery is that through the gospel the Gentiles are heirs together with Israel, members together of one body, and sharers together in the promise in Christ Jesus." (Ephesians 3:6). Though Christianity separated from its Jewish roots in later centuries, it retained so many Jewish practices even today, which was belonged to the time of Second Temple period. If we look at the structure of an Orthodox liturgy, we can see, it includes elements from the Second Temple functionaries of the temple such as readers, lectors, Levites, and singers, though not necessarily in same names. Other aspects we can notice from the Second Temple period are the antiphonal (singing alternative musical phrases by two groups) nature of ancient Christian prayers. Even the Church has adopted ceremonial actions from the Jewish liturgy such as processions and prostrations.

The Liturgical Connections:

The very foundation of the early liturgy originated in Jewish religious practices, as the early Apostolic Church preserved and maintained many of the liturgical form of Jewish worship. In reconstructing the Jewish background to Christian worship, Paul Bradshaw notes that:

> [i]n our efforts to assess the influence of Jewish practices upon Christian worship we ought to focus primarily upon the first century. It is true that contact between Jews and Christians did not end after 70 AD, and there is evidence for some continuing links down to at least the fourth century; some of the early Fathers were clearly influenced by Jewish sources, and John Chrysostom tells us that some ordinary Christians were attending both synagogue and church, though it is not clear how widespread, geographically or chronologically, this practice was.[18]

The tradition of the Church and the Scriptures teach us how the Eucharist began in the upper room at the Last Supper, as recounted in all four Gospels (see Matt 26:17–30, Mark 14:12–26, Luke 22:7–23, and John 13:1–20) and how the early Church obeyed Jesus's command to "break bread" in his name (Acts 2:42). But how was this memorial meal transformed into the highly ritualistic Eucharistic service it is today? Josef Jungmann suggests a theory of the development of the Eucharist in the first century:

"The Apostles fulfilled the command of our Lord given them at the Last Supper by celebrating

---

[18] Bradshaw, *Search for the Origins of Christian Worship,* 33.

regularly in the setting of a meal which was conducted with the ritual forms of Jewish community meal."[19] The supper meal included blessings over the bread and wine, the breaking of the bread, and *koinonia,* a Greek word which first occurs in Acts 2:42 and which means "fellowship, sharing in common, communion." The basic structure of the first part of the liturgy was apparently adapted from the Jewish evening service for the Sabbath that was celebrated at the time of our Lord.

The essential elements included an opening greeting, followed by a lesson from the Scripture. Immediately after that followed the Psalmody and a lesson. The sermon was next, and then followed the dismissal of the non-baptized, consisting of prayers and dismissal. The earliest evidence of such a structure is from the *First Apology* of Justin Martyr, as summarized by Paul Bradshaw in the following passage:

> Justin Martyr writing at Rome in the middle of the second century merely says "the records of the apostles or the writings of the

---

[19] Josef Jungmann, SJ, *The Mass of the Roman Rite: Its Origins and Development (Missarum Sollemnia)* (New York: Benziger Bros, 1959), 9.

> prophets are read for as long as time allows. Then, when the reader has finished, the president in a discourse admonishes and exhorts [us] to imitate these good things. Then we will stand up together and offer prayers...."[20]

Many scholars thus indicate that the first part of the liturgy was developed, more or less, from the Jewish meal service. Because of the steady growth of the community, these table prayers were transformed into a larger communal setting as Jungmann explains:

> The growing communities became too large for these domestic table-gatherings ... . Tables disappeared from the room, except for the one at which the presiding official pronounced the Eucharist over the bread and wine. The room was broadened into a large hall capable of holding the whole congregation. Only in isolated instances was the connection with the meal continued into the following centuries.[21]

---

[20] Bradshaw, *Origins of Christian Worship,* 123.

[21] Jungmann, *The Mass of the Roman Rite*, 10.

By the second century, primitive expressions like "breaking the bread" and "Lord's Supper" were replaced by the term "Eucharist," as seen in the writings of Ignatius of Antioch (107 AD)[22] and Justin Martyr (165 AD)[23]. There were few innovations in the celebration of the liturgy such as "inclusion of gifts brought by the faithful" and adding "milk and honey" for the newly baptized. However, more or less, the structure of the liturgy remained the same.

Passover and Ancient Christianity:

The early Christian writers, both inside and outside of the New Testament compared the Eucharistic celebrations in terms of the Passover. Historically, this idea was rooted in the Jewish hope for a messianic Passover and in the actions of Jesus himself. In the Book of Revelation, disciple John has a vision of Jesus in heaven. What John sees, however is not a man but a *Lamb* standing as though slain (Revelation 5:6) and through this Lamb the believers are made " into Kingdom and Priests into God." This strongly suggests that the heavenly worship

---

[22] "Letter to the Smyrnaeans", paragraph 6, circa 80-110A.D.

[23] "First Apology", Ch.66, inter A.D. 148-155.

surrounding this Lamb is not just any liturgical celebrations, but a heavenly Passover. Equally striking is the Saint Paul's writing to Corinthians, " For Christ, our Passover lamb, has been sacrificed." (1 Corinthians 5:7). Justin Martyr, writing in the Second century declares, " The mystery of the lamb, then, which God ordered you to sacrifice as the Passover, was truly a type of Christ." (Dialogue with Trypho, 40:1-3). The Catholic Church in its Catechism says, " Jesus passing over to his father by his death and Resurrection, the new Passover, is anticipated in the Supper and celebrated in the Eucharist, which fulfills the Jewish Passover and anticipates the final Passover of the Church in the glory of the Kingdom" (CCC 1339-1340). The New Testament, the Church Fathers and the teaching of the Catholic Church today, make it abundantly clear that the Last Supper- and, by extension, the Christian Eucharist- are nothing less than the new Passover of Messiah of the Jewish eschatological hope.

The Pharisaic Roots of the Early Church:

Some of the teachings of Jesus and Paul can be compared with the background of School of Hillel and Shammai of the first century AD. The theologian Marcello Del Verme argues that "Christianity and the New Testament are rooted in Judaism and he examined the Pharisaic roots of Jesus". At the time of Jesus and early Christianity, there are two leading Pharisaic scholars Bet Hillel and Bet Shammai made a mark on Judaism of their day. The major source of oral law is the result of debates between these two that is eventually found its way into the Mishnah (2nd century) and Talmud (fifth century). Hillel and Shammai are two divergent schools extremely opposite on defining Law and customs. They also differed in their attitude towards Gentiles and bring them to the Salvation. The school of Hillel supported for the outreach of Gentiles and brings them part of the overall salvation offered by God, which is also the cornerstone of Jesus's teachings. The sharp rebukes against the Pharisees seen in the Synoptic are those aligned with the school of Shammai who are radically oppose such outreach and enforce stricter worshipping rules. (Vermes 1984:86-87).

Essenism:

Recent discovery of the Dead Sea scrolls had shed some light over the life, thoughts and practices of a Jewish cult called Essenes who used to live in caves along the Dead Sea. After studying these scrolls, many theological scholars came up with theories connecting early Christians to the Essenes. The French historian, Ernest Renan, even took a position that Christianity began as a sort of Essenism. I have summarized few interesting parallels from these studies connecting Essenes and early Christians. The primitive Christianity added something essentially new, in contrast with its Jewish origins. The Jewish sect called itself, among other things, the " New Covenant." Also they called themselves as " Poor" which is a proper name for this group. We also find this term in the New Testament for the first Christians. The common meal of the Qumran sect exhibits much similarity to the Eucharistic feast of the first Christians. Essenes also "break the bread" and proclaim the presence of Messiah. The act of 'baptism' is a rite of initiation among the Essenes, which in certain sense, similar to the Christian baptism. In the Essene sect the community of goods is obligatory and organized s similar to the Apostolic time of Ananias and Sapphira. The Johannine dualism of Light and Darkness, Life and Death has its parallel in the Qumran texts. According to K.G. Kuhn "the body of the thought of the Qumran sect is very much in common as of the fourth Gospel. Corresponding to the prologue, they have a passage in the Rule (xi. II), where the divine thought appears as mediator of creation. The sin and grace is the theme seen in both New Testament and Qumran scrolls. There is one possible way to explain these similarities may have to do with the John the Baptist who is very much closer to these Essene sects. The disciples of John the Baptist became the early followers of Jesus.

The synagogue and church architecture:

> *"Pope Benedict XVI notes in his book "Spirit of the Liturgy" that in Christian sacred architecture, which both continues and transforms synagogue architecture, the Torah shrine has its equivalent in the altar at the east wall or in the apse, thus being the place where the sacrifice of Christ, the Word incarnate, becomes present in the liturgy of the Mass".*

One of the characteristics of Pope Benedict XVI's theology of the liturgy is his emphasis on the Jewish roots of Christian worship, which he considers a manifestation of the essential unity of Old and New Testament, a subject to which he repeatedly calls attention. Late Cardinal Ratzinger(Pope Benedict XVI)(1927-2022) and French theologian Louis Bouyer (1913-2004), did so many research on Liturgy and Architecture of Jewish and Christian worship centers. In Liturgy and Architecture, the famous French theologian explores the Jewish background to early church architecture, especially with regard to the "sacred direction" taken in divine worship. He notes that Jews in the Diaspora prayed towards Jerusalem or, more precisely, towards the presence of the transcendent God (shekinah) in the Holy of Holies of the Temple. Even after the destruction of the Temple the prevailing custom of turning towards Jerusalem for prayer was kept in the liturgy of the synagogue. Thus Jews have expressed their eschatological hope for the coming of the Messiah, the rebuilding of the Temple, and the gathering of God's people from the Diaspora. The direction of prayer was thus inseparably bound up with the messianic expectation of Israel. ….

Bouyer observes that this direction of prayer towards the Holy of Holies in the Temple of Jerusalem gave Jewish synagogue worship a quasi-sacramental quality that went beyond the mere proclamation of the word. This sacred direction was highlighted by the later development of the Torah shrine, where the scrolls of the Holy Scripture are solemnly kept. The Torah shrine thus becomes a sign of God's presence among his people, keeping alive the memory of his ineffable presence in the Holy of Holies of the Temple. Ratzinger notes in his book Spirit of the Liturgy that in Christian sacred architecture, which both continues and transforms synagogue architecture, the Torah shrine has its equivalent in the altar at the east wall or in the apse, thus being the place where the sacrifice of Christ, the Word incarnate, becomes present in the liturgy of the Mass. This is a clear continuation of Jewish architecture and beliefs in Christian worship places.

Conclusion:

The evolution of Christianity and its liturgy is very much indebted to the Second Temple period of Judaism. Christianity began life as a kind of Judaism, which, like that of the Dead Sea Scroll sectarians and the Samaritans. In the first century it spread not only among Palestine Jews but also among Jews in diaspora. The elements that were absorbed in Christian theology and worship evidently sprang from this period. Early Christian rituals and liturgical practices described in the New Testament or in the writings of Church Fathers are similar to the practices in both the early and later Jewish mainstream and sectarian rites. The number of such practices did not develop independently of Judaism. A sizable number of liturgical fragments from the Dead Sea Scroll reveal an organized prayer ritual. This material from Qumran indicates that although forms of Jewish prayer are thought to have been fluid at this time, it is clear that the building blocks of much of the future structure of the Jewish prayer is already in place. The members of the various Jewish Sects who became Christians bring their practices, rituals and prayers to Christianity. Sources indicate that worshippers reciting those prayers at their home and synagogues exactly same hour as in the temple worship. The early Christians retain the elements from these synagogue liturgies and the common worship of the first Christians and Jews was weakened with the fall of the Temple. Also the growth of the non-Jewish membership of Christianity, and quickly began to outnumber Christians of Jewish origin, its Christology became less inhibited by the constraints of Jewish monotheism. Judaism, with its stress on monotheism, could not accept the divinity of Christ that led further alienation of Jews from Christians by the end of the first century. Further it was Christianity's doctrinal position on the Jesus that eventually made worship together of Christians and Jews untenable.

Chapter 4: Education Through Liturgy.

The Christian Faith is not a philosophy, nor merely a morality of life. It is centered and given as a new church life by Christ. A redeemed sect through the baptism who received the mercy from God and constantly participating in the passion of Christi and in his resurrection. The sacraments enlighten and hold into the Body of Christ, i.e., the Church. Through the participation in the liturgy, we are entering into the communion with Word of God. The Faith of the Syrian Orthodox Church is built on three fundamental stones-Scripture, Teachings of the Church Fathers and the Tradition of the Church. Throughout the centuries, the church's medium of educating its faith is Church itself. The school theology is a western idea borrowed by the Church in the latest centuries. A rupture between the theological studies and liturgical experience is widely seen in the West especially in the Catholic Church today (Schememann 1986: 10). Present day worship is taught in schools as part of the ecclesial education or in the historical development of worship. The problem is such historical narrative of liturgy is not an objective understanding of the real nature of worship. Though the modern schools able to develop a liturgical discipline to be taught exclusively about the historical development of liturgy, the student's understanding of its real meaning is lacking. The Second Vatican Council came up with term *participation actuosa* which means "active participation". In the Catechism of the Catholic Church points out that "the word "liturgy" speaks to us of a common service and thus has a reference to the whole holy People of God" (VVV 1069). In the Eucharistic Liturgy we do an active participation through verbal praises and singing, responding through sign the cross, by folding our arms, prostrating, participating in hymns, observing signs and symbols and giving reverence to the Gospel and Holy Elements. Late Pope Benedict XVI correctly summarizes as follows "True liturgical education cannot consist in learning and experimenting with external activities. Instead, one must be led toward the essential *action* that makes the liturgy what it is, toward the transforming power of God" (Ratzinger 2000: 175). Internal participation is an essential criterion for transforming ourselves through liturgy.

The church imparted its teachings to the generations through the active participation in its liturgical services. The famous quote from the Church Father Tertullian (C.165-225) "Christians

We Believe in One True God-51

are made not born" (Apol.,xviii). In the early days of Christianity, Lenten time is organized in such a way that the catechumens receive biblical and liturgical education and knowledge of Chris through participation. In the early church, the baptism of catechumens took place during the night service in the night preceding Easter. So te Lent is the time for intense preparation to receive the "Sacrament of Enlightment" which is the Baptism, the first sacrament. The Baptism not just entrance to the Holy Church but the beginning of knowledge about Christ as the Holy Spirit is dwelling on the newly baptized through the Holy Oil. The baptism is the new beginning in their lives and old person is died as immersed in the baptismal pond and the new person is born again as they emerge from the baptismal pond.

The scripture readings during the Lent is mainly taken from Book of Genesis, Book of Isaiah and from the Proverbs. The purpose of such readings is arranged so that the Catechumens gained the knowledge about the foundation of everything this world is for. It is a microcosm of the scripture as whole and its purpose. By reading the Book of Genesis, a sound understanding about the Creation, God's love, Sin, the purpose of creation and the expectations. The Book of Genesis also dealt with the man's disobedience, Fall and the punishment, curse, flood and covenants. A sound knowledge about the Sovereign God, the nature of Creation and the cause of its ruin is gained through the pages of the Book of Genesis. Meantime in the Book of Isaiah, the readers get familiarize the theme of messianic promise, image of Messiah and the suffering servant. This will prepare the readers for the Holy Week where the Christ's suffering is the main focus in the Holy Week prayers. The Proverbs provide a good knowledge about the human wisdom, experience and knowledge about the divine wisdom and the theme of incarnation.

During the Holy Week, the readings shifted to the Book of Exodus and to Book of Job. The Exodus highlights the journey of the chosen people to the promised land, the great event of Passover which fulfills with the Christ (John 13:1) and Christ become our Passover Lamb (1 Cor. 5:7). By reading through the Book of Job, the reader reaches the pinnacle of their religious exposure as the Job is providing the climax of the Old Testament narratives. The revelation of the suffering servant who conquers evil with his humility, love and obedience of God. This is providing a suitable stage for self-evaluation and repentance. The tone, ambience and the solemn atmosphere during the Lenten time and the order of the readings, hymns and prayers, really calls for repentance, receiving the Word of God through scriptures and internal

We Believe in One True God-53

participation through the liturgy. So this is best time for a catechumen to actively practice and participate what he was taught all these time.

The Eucharistic Service has components that is composed in such a way that it is all connected to one another and slowly and gradually elevating the participants to the full participation and redemption through liturgy. The Eucharistic Service begins with the readings from the Old Testament, the Psalmody, the Epistles and finally the reading of the Gospel. The purpose of the readings before the Gospel is to prepare ourselves for the sacrament of the Word of God. This is followed by a sermon explaining the content and meaning of the Gospel reading of the day. The reading of the Gospel and its explanation through a sermon not just an insert into the liturgy but led to participants and prepare them to "come together" for the Holy Eucharist. So liturgy is not just an interesting custom but ancient way of educating the catechumens and the faithful. The meaning of this education is not just attaining the knowledge but bring the faithful in to the life of the Church to edify. It is an active participation through education. "O taste and See how good the God is" (Psalm 34:8). The scripture inviting us first taste God then See or understand Him. The participants in the liturgy unconsciously inhale and assimilate even before they fully understood the meaning of the liturgy.

The modern "Sunday School" system is a modern concept and more or less attributed to reformation movement. The concept is very much connected to the secular education. This way of teaching is contradicting the faith and belief of the ancient churches. The Syrian Orthodox Church and more or less all ancient churches believes that the Sunday should be a liturgy-centered day. The modern-day Sunday school teachings are more or less storytelling and folklore taken from the Old Testament events such as Noa's ark, Flood, Abel and Cain, Exodus etc. Such topics are selected more or less to gain attention to the young minds. The problem is such textbook stories failed to connect the real meaning what they have with the Sacraments. The failed to connect, for example, Flood and Baptism or Oil and Holy Spirit etc. Without knowing the themes and the meanings of water, oil and Holy Spirit in the Old and New Testaments, the waters of flood, the Passover and exodus are meaningless for the students and remain as Old testament stories in their minds. The water in the baptism represents both death as well as life. According to St. Cyril of Jerusalem, it is a grave and a birth giver. Water and Oil is also a sign for the future assurance of resurrection from the death. In the Eucharist, the bread and wine, body and blood of

We Believe in One True God-55

Christ or mixed bowl of milk and honey in olden days, represents fulfillments of Moses's promised land and enter into the new covenant. These meanings should be connected with the readings of the Exodus. Every sacramental sign are reminders of final consummation or second coming as it is proclaimed in the Gospel. Without knowing the meaning, participating in the liturgy of baptism is meaningless. Eucharist itself is the sign of Christ's passion, death and instituted for the final resurrection. The teaching of the Great Flood has no value in it. In order to contemplate and participate in the Holy Mysteries, especially during the Holy Week, the meaning and understanding of the Old Testament readings is essential.

Equally important is the Christological meanings in the liturgy. The overall themes in the liturgy such as blessings, thanksgiving, repentance, petition and sacrifice are all related to the spiritual meanings and dimensions. Their meanings and dimensions are given in the scriptures, but it is only through the liturgy they came alive in its unique and actual sense. Afterall, the liturgy and the enactments in the liturgy, reflect the belief of the Church by an articulation of the eternal truth in words, rituals and thorough music.

Understanding of the various signs used in the Liturgy is also very much important to get a full knowledge of what we are observing during the worship. The liturgical symbolism is very much rooted in the scriptures. The Mystery, who is Christ, is presented in the Scriptures, in the Church and in her Sacraments. The outward reality is concealed an inner spiritual reality. The Eucharist banquet is a symbol of union of the Soul with the divine Word of God. The altar itself is a symbol of our interior worship. The connection between physical and spiritual in terms of "bodily plane" is very strong which the modern man or Sunday school system has difficulty to grasp. It is absorbed only through active participation in the liturgy. The medium of spiritual expressions consists not only of our words but our gestures as well- interior participation with exterior signs. Reflection and participation in the liturgy can lead to an articulation of beliefs. The liturgy did not determine the beliefs but bear witness to it.

Chapter 5: Lex Orandi, Lex Credendi

Lex Orandi, lex credenda is a Latin word that became something of a tenet of liturgical theology. It is translated literally from Latin, which means "the law of what is prayed is the law of what is believed. It is further expanded to *lex orandi, lex credenda, lex vivendi* means the law of what is prayed is what is believed is the law of what is lived which is a motto in Christian tradition. The prayer and belief are integral to each other and the liturgy is not distinct from theology. It refers to the theological relationship between worship and belief.

In the Early Church, there was a liturgical tradition before there was a common creed and before there was an officially sanctioned biblical canon. We, the Orthodox, profess our faith through liturgy. Christians don't worship because they believe. They believe that the One in whose gift faith lies is regularly met in the common act of worship. Worship is the first articulation of our faith: the liturgy engages belief in a way that simply thinking about god. In other words, in the act of worship, the faithful are in a dialogue with the God and are engaged in an active and personal participation in relationship with Jesus Christ.

Worship is one way of praising God, an act that man and all other creatures partake in it. Also, worship is not an individual act meaning that each person separately praises and worships God, but rather, it is a public or community act. The church called this community worship liturgy. Liturgy also can be defined as the set of rituals by which the public worship of God is performed, and it can be connected to many life events such as birth, marriage, sickness, or death. Liturgy is a way we profess our faith.[24]

The final clause of the quotation, "that the order of supplication determines the rule of faith," is found in Latin as: "*ut legem credendi lex statuat supplicandi.*" The common interpretation of the adage holds that the content of prayer is synonymous with the faith of the one praying, such that we can understand the faith of the church by examining the liturgical rubrics in use at any particular time. The *lex orandi* `the law of prayer,` is thus understood to be the prescribed liturgical text, which serves as a

---

[24] Jesson, Nicholas. *Lex Orandi, Lex Credendi Towards a liturgical Theology* (Toronto. University of St. Michaels's College. 2001)12.

theological lens to interpret the *lex credendi*, the doctrinal standards.[25]

If by *lex orandi, lex credendi*, one is to establish which comes first, then obviously, according to Dr. Joseph Varghese,[26] *lex credendi* must come first chronologically. For how can one pray if one does not first believe? By definition, prayer is an act of faith, and hence faith must come first. Hence Pope Pius XII could declare in *Munificentissimus Deus*: "the liturgy of the Church does not engender the Catholic faith, but rather springs from it, in such a way that the practices of the sacred worship proceed from the faith as the fruit comes from the tree…[27] or as *lex orandi* articulates the faith from which prayer is engendered.

However, the words of Prosper of Aquitaine must be studied in their context if a just and academically honest understanding were to be reached, and an

---

[25] Jessen N. 7.

[26] Joseph Varghese, "Lex Orandi.mov" at *Sophia University*, last updated on February 8, 2021.

[27] Pius XII, *Munificentissimus Deus*, (Vatican City: Libreria Editrice Vaticana, 1950), 20.

evaluation of its influence can be ascertained. The context in which *ut legem credenda lex statuat supplicandi* occurs is Prosper's argument on grace and the "inviolable decisions of the blessed Apostolic See" and (*ut*) equating the *lex supplicandi* with the *legem credenda*. It seems to include the manner and content of prayer that is equal to doctrine (articulated faith). Here it is important to differentiate inarticulate faith from articulate faith. An infant or child below the age of reason is baptized while having inarticulate faith. The *lex orandi* necessarily follows after the inarticulate faith and will serve to articulate it. The *ut* is either a consecutive conjunction with temporal value or an explicative conjunction, which, either way, puts the *lex supplicandi* after the faith, even though it and faith are both equally "transmitted by the apostles."[28] It presupposes that one first has faith in the apostles' teachings, otherwise, articulated faith or prayer makes no sense.

Jesson rightly asserts that "The notion that liturgy supplies normative direction to theology is a methodological principle. To suggest that theology determines the norms for liturgy is a canonical

---

[28] Prosper Aquitanus, "Praeteritorum Sedis Apostolicae Episcoporum Auctoritates", Capitulum VIII *alias Cap. XI,* in *Patrologiae Cursus Completus (Series Latina 51)*, ed. by Jacques-Paul Migne, (Paris, 1861), 209.

principle." When these two levels of fundamental principles are recognized as essential dynamics, then *lex orandi, lex credendi* can then be understood in a symbiotic relation, which may work in both directions, the former elucidating the latter and vice versa. It occurs on different levels of principle and does not contradict sacred Tradition nor threaten theological logic. Moreover, in Latin grammar *lex orandi lex credendi* does not need a verb, and by grammatical rules, it can also mean *lex credendi lex orandi*. Latin, unlike Greek, does not put emphasis nor priority on first-position words in a phrase.

Perhaps asking which comes first in *lex orandi lex credendi* is a problem that results from a diachronic approached employed by many liturgical theologians following Aiden Kavanagh[29], who has been criticized by Michelle Gilgannon[30]. A synchronic approach, as adopted by Jesson, could be the solution.

---

[29] Aiden Kavanagh, *On Liturgical Theology*, (Collegeville: Liturgical Press, 1984).

[30] Michelle Gilgannon, *The Liturgical Theology of Aiden Kavanagh: Synthesis and Critique, A Dissertation*, Duquesne University, last updated in Fall 2011, https://dsc.duq.edu/cgi/viewcontent.cgi?article=1597&context=etd

If one were to see the relation between *lex orandi* with *lex credendi* in the liturgy today, then the gestures (*actio orandi*) must be understood with its verbal content (*verba orandi*). They are the form and matter of liturgical action. The gestures must be interpreted symbolically as they essentially are symbols, as Varghese's essay indicates. Signs and symbols are a form of language that intensifies the meaning of the liturgy and makes Christians easy to understand the underlying message in each act of worship.

An example in the Roman rite is the elevation of the Sacred Species. Already found in the time of the *Apostolic Constitutions*,[31] a form of elevation is practiced in all the ancient liturgies, though it is placed at different parts of the liturgies with different meanings. In the Roman Rite, it is placed at the Eucharistic doxology and before the Lord's Prayer. The Armenian Rite places an elevation between the Lord's Prayer and the Doxology before communion, as is also found in the Byzantine Liturgy of John Chrysostom.

In the Roman Rite, the Eucharistic doxology "Per ipsum et cum ipso et in ipso" is the triumphal

---

[31] *Apostolic Constitutions*, Book VIII, v, in New Advent, last updated 2020,

conclusion of the Eucharistic Prayer and is accompanied by the elevation of the Sacred Species. The Eucharistic doxology stands independently from the Eucharistic Prayer's preceding intercessions and is an offering up of Christ's sacrifice and his accomplished salvific work that glorifies him with the Father in unity with the Spirit. The consecrated host and wine in the chalice are lifted up high above the altar as the doxology is proclaimed or sung.

This elevation of the consecrated host and chalice is already attested in the 9th century or earlier in the Roman Rite.[32] The new directives and rubrics of the General Instruction of the Roman Missal in 2010, reserve "elevation"[33] only at this doxology and not during the offertory of gifts or before communion ("holds it slightly raised" or "shows").[16] These two latter actions have been called "elevations" prior to the liturgical reform of Vatican II but have now been corrected, thus leaving only one moment of true elevation, which is at the Eucharistic doxology.[17]

---

[32] Herbert Thurston, "The Elevation", in *The Catholic Encyclopedia*, last updated on 2020,

[33] General Instruction of the Roman Missal" 151, 180 *The Holy* See, last updated 2010,

By "elevation," the Congregation for Divine Worship and the Discipline of the Sacraments wanted to preserve the original meaning of "ana – phora" (raising up/elevation), which is properly this part of the liturgy. The "raising up/elevation" of the Sacred Species as the accomplished sacrifice of Christ culminates the Anaphora proper through gesture. This elevation offers up this sacrifice through ("per") and in Christ to be glorified with ("cum") the Father and the Spirit.

On the other hand, the *showing* of the Sacred Species before communion in the Roman rite corresponds to the Byzantine (Chrysostom) "Ta hagia tois hagois" and Armenian "Ee surpotyoun surpotz" which precedes the doxology, and is properly a *showing* of the Sacred Species to the faithful before they come forward to receive them, rather than an elevation of the sacrifice in glorification of the Trinity. The doxology glorifying the Trinity in the Armenian rite "Orhnootyoun yev park Hor" occurs later but does not have an elevation. The Byzantine (Chrysostom) rite lacks this.

In the Roman Rite, the Elevation is considered the climax of the Eucharistic Prayer, and is responded by the "Great Amen" of the faithful, a climax of offering back to the Father with the Spirit what the Father had offered to us in the first place – the redemptive sacrifice of his Son. Underlying this gesture of raising up/elevating/offering up is the soteriological and eschatological belief reflected in John 3:14 "Just as Moses lifted up the snake in the wilderness, so must the Son of Man be lifted up"; John 12:32 "When I am lifted up from the earth, I will draw all men to myself"; and indeed the entire portion of John 12:27-33.

Here, the theme of "lifting up" is associated with glory, judgment, drawing all people and the manner of death Christ was to endure. In John's gospel, it is the moment of supreme glory when and how Christ died – by being "lifted up" on the cross. The doctrinal tenets of soteriology and eschatology are encompassed in this gesture of "lifting up." It is soteriological because it describes the manner of death (atonement); it is redemptive because it draws all people to Christ (recapitulation/anakephalaiosis). It is eschatological because it brings judgment, which St. Paul warns regarding eating and drinking the Body and Blood of Christ.[34] And the glorification of the Trinity by Christ's obedience unto death, echoing what St. Paul said to the Philippians in Phil 2:8-9; is an "already-but-not-yet" eschatology, which is the glory of the resurrection but also the eschatological glory when Hell and

---

[34] 1Cor 11:29.

Death are destroyed for good as prophesied in Rev. 20:14.

When viewed in the light of the Elevation of the Sacred Species, Christ is symbolically "raised up" on the Cross, fulfilling all that he had spoken in Jn 3:14 and 12:27-33. By placing the Elevation after the Institution narrative and epiclesis, the sacrifice of Christ would have already been effected by the power of the Holy Spirit, and hence the Elevation is fittingly an offering back of the salvific gift to the Father, an act that glorifies the Trinity because creation is now made pristine again. This Elevation expresses all the soteriological and eschatological tenets of faith. In a visual way, it speaks theologically to the faithful as like a catechism.

But this *actio orandi* must be understood with the accompanying doxology, which is the *verba orandi*. The first part, "per ipsum et cum ipso et in ipso" is found at the end of the preceding intercessions in the Armenian and Byzantine (Chrysostom) anaphoras. The second part, "omnis honor et gloria" is found in the Greek acclamation "heis agios heis kyrios ..." and Armenian "miyayn surp miyayn Der ..." (but without the "honor," following the *Apostolic Constitutions*).[35] Responding to the "Holy Things

---

[35] *Apostolic Constitutions*, Book VIII, xiii.

for Holy People". Whether the Latin doxology is a combination of the two parts found in the Greek and Armenian usage or the Greek and Armenian versions divided the Latin prayer, or simply all three shared a common source is immaterial. The Latin doxology expresses the climactic consequence of Christ's salvific sacrifice, which is glorification of the Trinity by re-establishing all things in himself[36] and in this fullness, he fills all in all.[37] Creation comes to a full circle. The Trinitarian doctrine is enhanced by the Christological *pleroma*, uniting the creator with creatures again as back in the Garden of Eden, a recapitulation / *anakephalaiosis* which glorifies the Trinity.

The law of what is prayed is the law of what is believed, but we can hardly claim that we truly understand all that we believe in. This is where faith plays a major role, it opens up our hearts and minds so that we receive enlightenment through the grace given to us by Christ through the sacraments. Once again, we cannot receive this enlightenment through our own human understanding, it takes faith. Late Pope Benedict XVI explained the relationship between our understanding of the faith and

---

[36] Eph 1:10

[37] Eph 1:22-23

sacraments, saying, "The Church's faith is essentially a eucharistic faith, and it is especially nourished at the table of the Eucharist. Faith and the sacraments are two complementary aspects of ecclesial life. Awakened by the preaching of God's word, faith is nourished and grows in the grace-filled encounter with the Risen Lord, which takes place in the sacraments: "faith is expressed in the rite, while the rite reinforces and strengthens faith.[38]

Lex orandi, lex credendi expresses concisely the relationship between the celebration of the liturgy in worship and the formation (catechesis) of the faithful. On the one hand, the liturgy proclaims, not only in word but in sign and symbol, the Word of God. The faithful, in celebrating the liturgy, profess their faith".[39] The faithful get to experience God personally through the mysteries. This deepens our understanding of Him and strengthens our faith. We are enlightened through the sacraments. "Those who prepare for and celebrate the liturgy, lex orandi, as well as those responsible for catechesis, lex credendi, need to trust that the sacraments can and will do so: that the living Word of God will inspire

---

[38] Rick Hilgartner, "Lex Orandi, Lex Credendi: The Word of God in the Celebration of the Sacraments," United States Conference of Catholic Bishops, September 20, 2009.

[39] Rick Hilgartner 4.

the faithful to more authentic Christian living, lex vivendi."[40]

How we pray shapes how we believe. "Worship reveals what we truly believe and how we view ourselves in relationship to God, one another and the world into which we are sent to carry forward the redemptive mission of Jesus Christ. How the Church worships is a prophetic witness to the truth of what she professes. Good worship becomes a dynamic means of drawing the entire community into the fullness of life in Jesus Christ.

The liturgy serves as both a reflection of theology and as a norm for theological articulation. Correctly understood, liturgical theology is part of the theological articulation of the faith. This distinguishes it from liturgical studies, which is a descriptive study. The ancient adage "*lex orandi, lex credendi*" is a central focus of the consideration of the relationship between liturgical theology and dogmatic theology. The way the adage has been understood and applied will give insight into the contemporary relationship between Liturgy and Theology.

---

[40] Ibid 4.

This very short part in the liturgy of St. Basil - which the Coptic Orthodox Church prays regularly – articulates a vital part of the Christian belief. This part reminds the believers of the first effects of sin on the human race that it separated man from God and put a veil between them to prevent man from communicating with God as his first condition, and this separation needed a reconciliation which was only done by the cross on which the incarnated Son of God was crucified. In other words, the law of belief determined the law of prayer, and the law of prayer articulated the law of belief. Another example of how faith shapes the prayers, and the prayers express the faith is the preparatory part before the institution prayers in the Coptic liturgy where the priest says:

> Through Your Only-Begotten Son, our Lord, God and Savior Jesus Christ, Who is of the Holy Spirit and of the Virgin saint Mary incarnated and became man, and taught us the way of salvation. He granted us the grace of rebirth from above, through the water and the Spirit. He made us a united people unto Him and purified us through Your Holy Spirit. He loved His own people of the world, and for our salvation, He gave Himself up to death which had possessed us, whereby we were bound and sold on account of our sins. He descended into Hades through the Cross. He rose from the dead on the third day; He ascended to the heavens and sat at Your right hand, O' Father; He appointed a day for retribution, whence He will

> appear to judge the world in equity and reward each one according to his deeds. (Anaphora of St. Basil).

Here the priest – using "the law of prayer," mentions the main dogmas that Christians believe in, reminding all the believers attending the liturgy. The "law of belief" of the Church is the Word Incarnate took human form by uniting manhood to himself; thus, from the virgin, God the Son took the incarnate state. His earthly life, Passion, and death are all real. As such, there is no reduction of his humanity in the liturgical tradition of the belief of the Church. This part also adds another dimension which is *"lex vivendi,"* or what is called "the law of what is lived." Thus, the believers who practice these rites and rituals must show a change in their life according to what they believe in and what they pray.

To sum up, the liturgy and its practices reflect the belief of the church through the articulation of the eternal truth in various ways, such as words, gestures, liturgical music and all other activities associated with it. The reflection of the liturgy can lead to the articulation of beliefs, but liturgy does not determine the belief. Rather, it witnesses it. Also, the articulation of belief influences the development of liturgy. For example, the initiation of what is happening in baptism is articulated from our belief and our faith in different places and different ways to celebrate when the church celebrates the sacraments. The believers confess their faith in the apostles and the Holy Tradition.

Finally, as there is no difference between God's words and His deeds, there should be no difference between man's faith extracted from the word and his contribution to the body of Christ through different liturgical practices; *lex credendi* influences *Lex orandi* leading to *lex vivendi.*

Chapter 6: The Christological Development through the Centuries.

Before investigating the Eucharistic Liturgy of the Syrian Orthodox Church, we must first examine that Church's Christological position. The Syriac Orthodox Church recognizes only the first three ecumenical councils: the First Council of Nicaea, the First Council of Constantinople, and the First Council of Ephesus. The Church rejects the definitions of the Council of Chalcedon, held in 451 A.D. in Chalcedon, as well as the teachings of both Nestorius and Eutyches. After the Council of Chalcedon (c. 451), the Syriac Orthodox Church, along with the Coptic Orthodox Church (both of which are known as Alexandrines), separated from the Byzantine and Roman Christians. In brief, the teachings and doctrine of the Syrian Orthodox Church present God Incarnate with his divinity and humanity fully present and united without mixture, confusion, or change. In this chapter, we will examine this Christology, particularly as formulated by the Church Father St. Cyril of Alexandria. As concerning two natures of Christ, the Church unwaveringly upheld the formula of St. Cyril of

Alexandria which was accepted by both Chalcedonian and non-Chalcedonian Churches equally. The Church kept St. Cyril's formula of "One nature of God the Logos incarnates which reveals the Hypostatic union of natures, the divine and the human in one without mingling, nor confusion, nor alteration." Even though the non-Chalcedonian Churches are wrongly accused with the Eutychianism, the Church has vehemently denied it since the very beginning and affirmably withstand with two natures of the Word incarnate.

The Christological position of the Church after the Council of Chalcedon can be viewed more or less as an expression of the union of the divine and human natures of Christ. The Oriental Orthodox concept regarding the "nature of Christ" has been well addressed by Pope Shenouda III of the Coptic Church:

> The divine and human nature was united in a hypostatic union, without mingling, confusion or alteration. God the Logos took flesh from the Holy Virgin and "the Holy Spirit purified and sanctified the Virgin's womb so that the Child to whom she gave

birth would inherit nothing of the original sin."[41]

"This unity of natures led to the formulation of 'The One Nature of God,' "says Pope Shenouda. Quoting St. Cyril of Alexandria, he continues, "As a result of the unity of both natures—the divine and the human—inside the Virgin's womb, one nature was formed out of both: 'The One Nature of God the Incarnate Logos,' as St. Cyril called it."[42]

Because of these expressions concerning the nature of Christ, the Syriac Orthodox Church, along with the Oriental Churches, was considered as being among the "Monophysite" churches, to use a term, which refers to the "one nature" of Christ. The Church suffered bitter clashes between the orthodox (Chalcedonians) and the strict Cyrillians (Monophysites), which eventually resulted in the first serious and abiding schism in the Church. This turmoil was painful for the Empire as well as the Church: the Monophysite schism fractured the Church, which was an important vehicle for political unity, and thus loosened the ties of the Empire with

---

[41] Shenouda III, *The Nature of Christ* (Cairo: Coptic Orthodox Patriarchate, 1991), 7.

[42] Ibid., 8.

the increasingly Monophysite Egypt and Syria, which were both vitally important for the Roman state. This Cyrillian Monophysitism was the conventional mode, which the majority of Eastern Christians were accustomed to use when describing the union of the two natures in Christ, the "one hypostasis" of the Logos incarnate. The Alexandrian theologians often understood the terms *physis*, *hypostasis*, and *prospone* as synonymous—that is, meaning the concrete being—and applied them interchangeably to the person of Christ. Because the Antiochene school always spoke about two hypostases in Christ in order to show the reality of the divinity and humanity of Christ, a division in understanding each other's positions arose, which deepened and eventually resulted in the first serious and abiding schism in Christendom. Modern scholarship has tried to explain these positions in terms of their soteriological aspects. Pope Shenouda asks whether the Oriental Churches that hold to Monophysite Christology believe in only one nature of Christ and deny the other:

> We wonder which of the two natures the Church of Alexandria denies. It cannot be the divine nature, since the Alexandrian Church fought against Arianism. According to Oriental Christology, "The expression One Nature does not indicate the divine Nature alone nor the human nature alone, but it

indicates the unity of both natures into One Nature which is the 'The Nature of the Incarnate Logos.'" It can be likened to the human nature, which is composed of two united natures - soul and body. The divine nature is hypostatically united with the human nature. The expression "two natures" suggests separation or division, and this was why the Coptic Church rejected Chalcedon, where the "tone of separation" was obvious.[43]

In its theology and liturgy, the Syriac Orthodox Church has always emphasized equally the divinity and the humanity of Christ. For example, at the Eucharistic preparation, the Church offers a mixture of wine and water. These represent the divinity and humanity of Christ, as seen in the accompanying prayer in the Anaphora of St. James: "Unite, Lord, this water with this wine even as thy divinity is united with our humanity."[44] It is interesting to see what St. Cyril himself wrote in his

---

[43] Shenouda III, *The Nature*, 4.

[44] "Anaphora of St. James," Syrian Orthodox Resources, last modified December 1, 1997, accessed March 10, 2017, http://sor.cua.edu/Liturgy/Anaphora/James.html.

letter to John of Antioch concerning this theological understanding:

> He (Christ) is also called the Man from heaven, being perfect in His divinity and perfect in His humanity, and considered as one of us in one Person (hypostasis). For One is the Lord Jesus Christ, although the differences of His natures are not unknown, from which we say the ineffable union was made.[45]

Obviously St. Cyril of Alexandria here recognizes the two natures in Christ incarnate, and he says in the same letter, "Will your holiness vouchsafe to silence those who say that a *crasis*, or mingling or mixture took place between the Word of God and the flesh? For it is likely that certain also gossip about me as having thought or said such things."[46]

The Fathers of the Church, including Cyril and Severus, always emphasized that the will of Christ is the will of the Father. *The Syriac Chronicle* of

---

[45] Cyril of Alexandria, *The Letter of Cyril to John of Antioch*, Found in Labbe and Cossart, Tom.IV., col. 343 and col. 164, ed. Philip Schaff and Henry Wace. The Nicene and Post-Nicene Fathers XIV, Second Series (Albany, OR: Sage Software, 1996), 616.

[46] Cyril, *The Letter of Cyril*, 616.

Michael Rabo (The Great), who lived in the early twelfth century, is a treatise emphasizing that the Armenians share with the Syrians the doctrinal faith of "One Nature of Christ," following the theological system of St. Cyril of Alexandria. As the Syrian Patriarch of Antioch, His Holiness Michael Rabo, writes:

> We do not say "one nature and one *qnumo* (hypostasis) for the divine and the human." We say that the composite Christ is one nature and one composite *qnumo* (hypostasis). For the composite …lacuna…that is …lacuna… we confess and worship one *qnumo* and it alone we worship without the one is loftier than the other or the one absorbed by the other …lacuna… We say that it has become consummate for both of them. We have rejected such ideas many times. Moreover, we consider as ridiculous the ideas of those who think that the union of the two natures might have been reversed or that it was subject to assimilation. Such a thing does not even happen to other compound matters.[47]

---

[47] Michael Rabo, *The Syriac Chronicle*, trans. Matti Moosa (Teaneck, NJ: Beth Antioch Press, 2014), 271.

In summary, the reason for the split in the Council of Chalcedon is that Christ was proclaimed "in two natures," which was resolutely affirmed as dyophysitism over monophysitism by the Alexandrian School. The Alexandrian School promoted the view that the divine and human natures were united in a hypostatic union, without mingling, confusion, or alteration after the union. Christ was held to be no longer in two natures, an idea that was denounced as the "dualistic" tendency of Antiochenes. The majority of the Christian East followed the Alexandrian formula of Cyril. The followers of Cyril of Alexandria were concerned about the intimacy of the union of the two natures; thus, they strove to safeguard the fact that Christ was a single subject, the Logos. In the hypostatic union, the humanity of Christ is never reduced or absorbed. The writings of St. Cyril confirm the Syriac Orthodox Church in following the Christology which affirms its position concerning Christ as perfectly divine and perfectly human. As a further reason for the split, the Alexandrians were critical of the hierarchical importance attached to Constantinople that received second place in ecclesiastical matters at the cost of the status of Alexandria, which had traditionally been a secondary consideration. Though attempts were made to rejoin the warring factions, imperial politics dominated over finding a resolution to the theological differences.

Christological Position agreed by the Syrian Orthodox and the Catholic Church

Ecumenical dialogue and a close understanding between the Catholic Church and the Oriental Orthodox Churches began after a series of consultation in a Pro Oriente meeting took place in Vienna in 1971. A bilateral consultation between the Catholic Church and the Syrian Orthodox Church began earlier; Pope Paul VI and Patriarch Mor Ya'qub III met in Rome in 1971and issued a joint declaration. The meeting was intended to narrow or eliminate theological differences and to recognize a common ground in relation to the faith, sacraments, and devotional practices of both Churches. This work was continued further through the annual consultations between two Churches on the local as well as at the highest levels. In 1984, a summit in Rome between the Patriarch Mor Ignatius Zakka I Iwas and Pope John Paul II took place, and an historic joint declaration was issued on matters of faith, sacraments, and the ecumenical relationship between two ancient Churches. The joint declaration notes the following regarding the discussion which took place at this meeting:

They denied that there was any difference in the faith they confessed in the mystery of the Word of God made flesh and become truly man. In our turn we confess that He became incarnate for us, taking to himself a real body with a rational soul. He shared our humanity in all things except sin. We confess that our Lord and our God, our Saviour and the King of all, Jesus Christ, is perfect God as to His divinity and perfect man as to His humanity. In Him His divinity is united to His humanity. This Union is real, perfect, without blending or mingling, without confusion, without alteration, without division, without the least separation. He who is God eternal and indivisible, became visible in the flesh and took the form of servant. In him are united, in a real, perfect indivisible and inseparable way, divinity and humanity, and in him all their properties are present and active.[48]

Thus, both prelates confessed that the faith of their respective Churches was formulated by the Council of Nicaea. Both Churches reaffirmed their common faith in the incarnation of Lord Jesus Christ and denied that there is any difference in the faith they confess in the mystery of incarnation of Word the God. The joint communiqué further clarified that

---

[48] "Common Declaration of Pope John Paul II and the Ecumenical Patriarch of Antioch HH Mar Ignatius I Iwas" (June 23, 1984), accessed March 11, 2017, at the Holy See,
http://w2.vatican.va/content/john-paul-ii/en/speeches/1984/june/documents/hf_jp-ii_spe_19840623_jp-ii-zakka-i.html

there was no real basis for the divisions and schisms between two Churches that occurred subsequently after the Council of Ephesus. The document also indicated that both Churches believed in the divinity and humanity of Christ and the union is "real, perfect, without blending or mingling, without confusion, without alteration, without division, without the least separation." In sum, the Pope and the Patriarch emphasized that the differences between the Chalcedon and non-Chalcedon Churches existed mainly because of alack of proper terminology that would enable both sides to express and understand fully each other's position. Both prelates agreed on four points: (1) unanimity on opinions on Christology, (2) willingness to collaborate mutually in priestly formation and pastoral care, (3) limited cooperation in the Sacraments (i.e., Penance [Confession], Eucharist, and Anointing of the Sick can now be received from either Church under certain circumstances), and (4) the desire to continue such contacts so that ultimately there could be full communion between the two churches.

Eastern Orthodox theologian Bishop Timothy Ware has written recently about the ecumenical relationship between the churches. He notes,

> A number of western and Orthodox scholars now believe that the Monophysite teaching about the person of Christ has in the past been seriously misunderstood, and that the difference between those who accept and those who reject the decrees of Chalcedon is largely if not entirely verbal…. The theological questions need to be seriously discussed, for the non-Chalcedonian Churches still feel a deep-rooted objection to the Chalcedonian Definition. Nonetheless, of all the "ecumenical" contacts of Orthodoxy, the friendship with the Monophysites seems the most hopeful and the most likely to lead to concrete results in the near future.[49]

In regard to the relations between the Catholic Church and the Oriental Orthodox Churches, Father Ronald Roberson, Associate Director of the Secretariat for Ecumenical and Interreligious Affairs at the United States Conference of Catholic Bishops, says,

> The Catholic-Oriental Orthodox relationship has already proved its importance by providing an example of how past disagreements over verbal formulas can be

---

[49] Timothy Ware, *The Orthodox Church* (Baltimore: Penguin Books 1963), 321.

overcome. This was not done by one side capitulating to the other, but by moving beyond the words of faith that those words are intended to express. Catholics and Oriental Orthodox now agree that, by means of different words and concepts, they express the same faith in Jesus Christ.[50]

The Protestant Churches are indebted by and large, their Christology to the Catholic Church. Most of these Protestant Churches including the Evangelicals confused the Oriental Orthodox Churches for Apollinarians and Eutychians. The Anglicans all along believed that the Oriental Orthodox Churches are "monophysite" until in 2014, they changed to " Miaphysite" in their agreed statement at the Joint Commission of Oriental Orthodox-Anglican Churches (https://www.anglicancommunion.org/media/103502/anglican-oriental-orthodox-agreed-statement-on-christology-cairo-2014.pdf). For some of the Protestants, the "one nature" stands for Christ is only partially (half) God and partially(half) human (Soetanto 2020). The leadership of the Evangelical

---

[50] Ronald Robertson "Relations between the Catholic Church and the Oriental Orthodox Churches," Catholic Near East Welfare Association/Resources, accessed on February 1, 2017, http://www.cnewa.org/resources.

Church maintaining a stereotype view against the Oriental Orthodox Churches because they believe the Oriental Orthodox churches are the heterodox because of their teachings on "Miaphysite" (Soetanto 2020). The modern Baptist theological students such as YSG Soetanto are more forthright in their research studies. He admits that the Christology of the Oriental Orthodox Churches is "Miaphysite"- one nature, perfectly God and perfectly human, without mixture, mingling or confusion (Soetanto 2020:2).

With the Eastern Orthodox Churches:

On the matter of Christological differences between Chalcedon and Non-Chalcedon Churches, the theologian Pelikan argued that the "cultural and semantic" differences contributed to understanding the Greek terms such as *physis, hypostasis, prosopon* by the Syrian speaking Churches (Pelikan 1974:37-8). The modern theological scholarship mislabeled the Syrian orthodox Church as the "followers of Eutyches" (Brock 1992:130). The confusion is based on the assumption of the modern scholars that the Syrian Orthodox Church hold the Christological position that Christ is in one person, which is definitely divine as compared to the Chalcedonian Churches position of Christ is one person with two natures.

There is no communion in large between the Eastern Orthodox and the Syrian Orthodox Churches. There are local initiatives taken by the local Church Councils such as the Middle Eastern Council of Churches to bring all churches together in an ecumenical platform. The official and unofficial dialogue between these two churches during the fifth, sixth and seventh centuries and compromised documents such as *heinoticon* by the Roman Emperor Zeno didn't yield much result in resolving the Christological controversaries. In 1964 the *Faith and Order* of the World Council of Churches met at Aarhus, Denmark and called for renewed cooperation, dialogue and unity among the member churches. In response to this call the theologians of Orthodox and Oriental Orthodox Churches met unofficially for the first time and each side formally recognized each other and their Orthodox faith. On the conclusion of these first consultation both groups found in agreement that the theological formula of Cyril of Alexandria expressed the same truth and believed in common unity though different terminology used in defining the "Mia physis" terminology (GOTR.vol.10.no.2 Winter 1964-65: 12-15). The theologians further agreed on "the full unity between the divinity and the humanity of Lord Jesus Christ" (Florescu 2019: 457). The two-nature formula of the Syrian Orthodox Church seen in its Christological debate with the Eastern Orthodox Churches. The Christological Consensus reached in Geneva at the Third and Fourth unofficial consultations between Oriental Orthodox and Eastern orthodox theologians in August 1970 in which the Syrian Orthodox Church theologian Poulose Gregorios stated:

> We know now that those who use the terminology of one nature want to give centrality to the fact of union. What is united in One. We know also that those who speak of two natures do not thereby seek to deny the unity of the person or the union of the natures. They are simply afraid that to speak of one nature may mean affirming *only (monos)* one of the two natures that were united. We know now that those who speak of One nature do not thereby deny the full and perfect humanity of Christ. We now know also that those who speak of two natures do not thereby mean that the humanity and divinity can exist separately or function one without the other (Aydin 2016: 298).

The Christological consensus agreed by these theologians forwarded a short formula of "The One unite divine-human nature of God" (Pro Oriente 1993: 177-183) as they hope to be acceptable to the Chalcedonian and Non-Chalcedonian churches.

Unfortunately the Church leadership hesitant to follow through and no head waves on dealing with these Christological differences achieved as of yet.

Chapter 7: Development of the Liturgy under the Church Fathers

The Christology of St. Cyril of Alexandria (376-444)

St. Cyril of Alexandria was the Patriarch of Alexandria and an exponent of Christological definitions. He was the central figure at the Council of Ephesus in 431 A.D., which resulted in the expulsion of Nestorius from the Patriarchate of Constantinople. Concerning the two natures of Christ, the Church unwaveringly upheld the formula of St. Cyril of Alexandria, which was accepted by both the Chalcedonian and non-Chalcedonian churches equally. The Syrian Orthodox Church kept St. Cyril's formula, in which he referred to the One Nature of God the Logos Incarnate, which reveals the hypostatic union of natures, the divine and the human in one without mingling, confusion, or alteration. The non-Chalcedonian Churches have been accused of Eutychianism, which they have vehemently denied because, since the very beginning, they have affirmed the two natures of the Word Incarnate. Father V.C. Samuel summarized this as follows:

We Believe in One True God-91

> The non-Chalcedon position affirms that God the Son, one of the blessed Trinity, united manhood to himself. In the union the manhood is not impersonal, though not a person parallel to the person of God the Son. He is a compound person, God the Son integrating in himself the personal reality of the manhood. Jesus Christ is therefore God the Son in his incarnate state, and as such the saviour of the world.[51]

In addition to this theological controversy, other reasons contributed to the rift between churches after the Council of Chalcedon. The political climate of the Eastern Roman Empire, the age-old bitter hatred between the Antiochene and Alexandrian theological schools, and a failure to grasp the complete meaning of terms used were all contributing factors leading to the split at the Council of Chalcedon in 451. Ecclesiastical politics came into play as well, both directly and indirectly. At the Council of Constantinople, the Council Fathers granted primacy of honor to the See of Constantinople, the new Rome. The Council of Chalcedon then became a venue for establishing the

---

[51] V. C. Samuel, *The Council of Chalcedon Re-examined* (Delhi: Indian Society for Promoting Christian Knowledge, 2001), 302.

interests of the Empire over the wishes of the Church of East. In order to win political advantage, it was necessary for the Empire to assert this primacy of Constantinople over the Church of Alexandria. Another factor of division between the Antiochean and Alexandrian schools was the extreme positions in the two divergent views of Nestorianism and Eutychianism regarding how to express Christ's divinity and humanity. This played a major role in the two sides' not understanding each other's position. The problem was viewed from mainly two angles corresponding to the basic schools of Christian thought at that time: 1) the Antiochene, which was represented by writers like Eustathius of Antioch c. 337), Diodore of Tarsus (c. 390) and Theodore of Mopsuestia (c.350–428), and 2) the Alexandrian, with Athanasius (c. 296–373) and Cyril of Alexandria (c. 375–444) on the orthodox, and Apollinarius on the heterodox, side. The Antiochenes, anxious to show the completeness of Christ's humanity and its significance for our salvation, spoke in terms, which allowed for a degree of autonomy for the human element in the Savior. If there is one doctrine that characterizes their Christology, it is the distinction between the two natures (Antiochene dyophysitism). The Alexandrians, on the other hand, were much more concerned with the intimacy of the union of the two natures and strove to safeguard that Christ was a single subject, the Logos.

Father V.C.Samuel, an eminent Church historian, provides an explanation of these distinctions:

> The position affirmed by the Nicene theologians in excluding Arianism answered only one side of the person of Christ. The other side referred to the question of how his life in the historical plane was to be understood. Acknowledging his personal unity, it was necessary to interpret his human reality without prejudice to his divine status. This important point had not been affirmed by the Alexandrine and the Antiochene leaders in the light of a uniform pattern in thinking. The west also had its tradition in dealing with this point, but it could accommodate the Antiochene heritage much more easily than that of the Alexandrines. All the three of them, however, would officially accept the Nicene Creed.[52]

St. Severus of Antioch (c.465-538)

St. Severus, Patriarch of Antioch, is revered as a great theologian of his time who expressed forcefully and clearly the Christology of St. Cyril.

---

[52] Samuel, *The Council of Chalcedon Re-examined*, 4.

St. Severus rejected both Nestorianism and Eutychianism, and articulated his Christology by quoting Cyril:

> For even if the Only-Begotten Son of God, incarnate and inhominate, is said by us to be one, he is not confused because of this, as he seems to those people, nor has the nature of the Word passed over into the nature of the flesh, nor indeed has the nature of the flesh passed into that which is his, but while each one of them continues together in the particularity that belongs to the nature, and is thought of in accordance with the account which has just been given by us, the inexpressible and ineffable union shows us one nature of the son, but as I have said, incarnate.[53]

In the period between 518 and 520 AD, St. Severus wrote three letters to a certain Sergius who was attempting to expound the Orthodox teaching of incarnation of Christ. In his writings to Sergius, St. Severus noted,

---

[53] Iain R. Torrance, *Christology After Chalcedon: Severus of Antioch and Sergius the Monophysite* (Norwich: Canterbury Press, 1988), 148.

> ...particularity implies the otherness of natures of those things which have come together in union, and the difference lies in natural quality. For the one is uncreated, but the other created... Nevertheless, while this difference and the particularity of the natures, from which comes the one Christ, still remains without confusion, it is said that [the]Word of Life was both seen and touched.[54]

The teaching of St. Severus had a major impact on articulating the Syrian Orthodox Church's position on Christology in the later years of her history. St. Cyril had repudiated any teaching in which the distinctions between the divine and human natures of Christ cease to exist in the Incarnation, as well as any teaching that damages the perfect reality of the divinity and humanity of Christ. That is, the Church believes in the one incarnate nature of the Word, and Christ is called "Emmanuel" because of the reality of his humanity, and because of his divinity: "He is with us." St. Severus clarified this in the following words:

> Before the union and the Incarnation, the Word was simple, not incarnate nor

---

[54] Ibid., 148.

composite. But when he mercifully willed in the dispensation to become man unchangeably along with being what He was, then He was called Christ as Emmanuel—the name being taken from the act—and He became one with us, by reason of the fact that He united to Himself in His Person (hypostasis) flesh which was of the same substance with us and which was animated with a rational and intelligent soul.[55]

For St. Severus, the divine hypostasis of the Word is eternal and is self-subsisting. By repudiating the Nestorian position, St. Severus denies any idea of the pre-existence of flesh prior to the Incarnation. But after the Incarnation, the flesh of Christ is true flesh; it is real and belongs to a complete individual, a fully human being. St. Severus explains that whereas the composition of the man Christ is made up of hypostatic elements, the elements are not self-subsistent: that is, though the humanity subsists, it is dependent on the union with the divine hypostasis, which is the Logos. Humanity alone cannot bear another person because it is not self-subsistent. Thus, the integrity of the complete humanity and complete divinity of Christ is always preserved in Severus' view. He also believes that the

---

[55] Torrance, *Christology After Chalcedon*, 149.

hypostatic union is "intrinsically redemptive"; that is, the Word became man to redeem humanity. Lastly, Severus often quotes Gregory and Cyril in emphasizing that "[t]he Word underwent real incarnation."[56] He teaches that the one nature of God the Word Incarnate should be understood as allowing two natures to continue to exist in the union of natures and to preserve their distinctions and characteristics. Thus, Severus supports the Christological position of Cyril of Alexandria, who confessed a union in which these real and different natures are united such that Christ is One, as the Nicene Creed professes.

St. Severus was also instrumental in revising the liturgy. The homilies of St. Severus are a rich source for details concerning everyday spiritual life and for examining the development of liturgical practices. The entrance chant of the liturgy ("By thy Mother's earnest plea….") is attributed to St. Severus, as are several other prayers:

1. The epiclesis and intercession of the Anaphora of Severus of Antioch.

2. The Prayer of Fraction of the Patriarch Severus.

---

[56] Ibid., 149.

3. A prayer of Severus used by the Coptic Church in the *Troparion*:

> O Only Begotten Son and the Word of God the immortal and everlasting, accepting everything for our salvation, the Incarnated from the Theotokos ever-Virgin Saint Mary, without change, Christ God becoming Man, crucified, through death treating death, one of the Holy Trinity to whom is glorification with the Father and the Holy Spirit, Save us.[57]

Today, the Syrian and the Coptic Churches remember St. Severus as the "crown of Syrians, the eloquent mouth, the pillar and the doctor of the Holy Church of God." He was a fascinating figure in the early Church who is remembered as simultaneously as both saint and heretic. He vehemently opposed the outcome of the Council of Chalcedon, and his work was condemned by imperial edict in 536AD. Though St. Severus is revered as a saint and leader of the Oriental Orthodox Churches, several councils have anathematized his doctrines on Christology. Today, the Greek and Roman Catholic Churches still maintain that positions of St. Severus were heretical.

---

[57] Youhanna Nessim Youssef, "Severus of Antioch in the Coptic Liturgical Books," *Journal of Coptic Studies* 6 (2004): 139–148.

Indeed, a renewed interest in Severus of Antioch is a key topic in current ecumenical dialogues with the Greek and Roman Catholic Churches.

Jacob Baradaeus (c.505–578)

The evolution of the Liturgy of St. James in the Syriac language continued after the Council of Chalcedon (c.451), and this liturgy became popular in remote areas where the Syriac language was spoken. Ishaq Saka, in writing about the Syriac Liturgy notes, "it is certain that many additions have been made to it through the course of time."[58] After the Council of Chalcedon, Emperor Justinian I resolved to enforce the decrees of the Council of Chalcedon by imprisoning and exiling those bishops and priests who did not accept the decrees of Chalcedon. The whole district of Syria and the adjacent provinces were deprived of any sacraments and threatened with eradication. With the help of Theodora (the Empress who was sympathetic to the non-Chalcedonian faction), Jacob was consecrated as a universal bishop with the assistance of three imprisoned bishops and the exiled Patriarch of Alexandria, Mor Theodosius. Bishop Jacob adhered to the Christology and faith of the first three ecumenical councils and rejected

---

[58] Saka, *Commentary on the Liturgy*, 2.

the decrees of the Council of Chalcedon. He upheld the doctrines of St. Cyril and supported the stand taken by Dioscoros at the Council of Ephesus. It is believed that Jacob Baradeus produced the first Syriac translation of the complete Greek text of the Anaphora of St. James. He also drew up a liturgy in fifteen pages beginning with, "O Lord, the most holy Father of peace." This liturgy, along with several of his letters—three of which are addressed to John of Ephesus—highlight the Christological position of the Church.

Liturgical Formulation under Various Church Fathers

The Liturgy of St. James underwent its first major revision under the celebrated theologian and reformer Jacob of Edessa (c.640–708),who revised the original Syriac material with the poetic compositions of St. Ephraim (c.373). The liturgical compositions of St. Ephraim are a key to unlocking the Christological mysteries expressed by the East. Many of St. Ephraim's writings became strong hymnographical and structural elements of the Syrian Orthodox liturgy. St. Ephraim used such language as "God the Son dwelt in humanity; God the Son wore humanity as a garment; God dwelt in the temple of man."[59] These phrases give us a clear view of St. Ephraim's Christological understanding of God putting on the garment of mankind by his Incarnation. The Church does not believe that St. Ephraim's verses reflect a nascent Docetism, but rather, that they affirm the divinity and humanity of Christ as an essential part of the salvation of humankind.

Jacob of Sarug (c.521) was also a celebrated doctor of the Church who composed liturgical hymns. He is known as the "flute of the Holy Spirit" and the "harp of the Church." The metrical hymn during the Fraction Rite is credited to Jacob of Sarug. This song used at the time the "Fraction rite" is addressed to the Father, who has offered his Son as the redeemer of mankind. The priest who is offering the sacrifice asks God to accept these offerings as a sacrifice: "Since the Son died for me, please accept my offerings." Jacob of Sarug's Christology can be identified with that of both Philoxenos of Mabbug and Severus of Antioch. Though Jacob did not participate directly in the Christological

---

[59] *The Book of Common Prayer Book of the Syrian Church*, trans. Bede Griffiths (Piscataway, NJ: Gorgias Press, 2005) 149-150.

controversies, his writings and exegesis express his Christological position.

In later years, the Syrian Church Fathers—like Moses Bar Kepha, Bishop of Mosul (c.813–903), and Bishop Dionysius Bar Salibi (c.1171)—lengthened the text with the Prayer of Fraction, including an expanded Rite of Fraction. Gregorios Bar Hebraeus (c.1286), a Syrian Church Maphrianite of the Persian Empire, abridged the text ascribed to Jacob of Edessa, thus giving the Church both a longer and a shorter version of the Liturgy of St. James. Subsequently the Syriac liturgy added seventy-nine anaphoras, all of which are attributed to various Apostles and Church Fathers.

It should be noted that the non-Chalcedonian Churches were mostly located in the geographical areas of Egypt, Syria, and Mesopotamia. The Byzantines, with their political power over Egypt and Syria, persecuted the non-Chalcedonian Churches with the blessing of the Chalcedonian Church.[60] The sudden rise of Islam early in the seventh century posed a new challenge to Persia and Byzantium as they had exhausted their resources, having fought each other for an entire century. At first, the non-Chalcedonian Christians welcomed the

---

[60] "History of the Coptic Church," The Coptic Orthodox Church Centre UK, accessed February 10, 2017, http://www.copticcentre.com/history.

advancing Arab armies, imagining they were their liberators! Ironically, these Christians had enjoyed more freedom than their fellow Christians of the West because they lived within the Persian Empire. The invading Islamic armies expected all pagan subjects to Islamize; but they did allow Jews and Christians to remain within their faith according to specific restrictions. The Arabs granted them the status of *Dhimmis*, an Arabic word that literally means "under the protection" of the new masters. In this way, the Muslims allowed these communities to survive under their control. There was a tendency by the non-Chalcedonian Christians to emphasize the "divinity of Christ" because it appeased their rulers and to promote the monotheistic idea of God more in their expression of Christ as fully divine and human.[61]

By the thirteenth century, additional liturgical revisions had been made in some parts of the region. Father Baby Varghese has said that in the liturgy of the Syrian Church, new elements were introduced, such as extended preparation rites, a dramatic blessing of the censor during the pre-anaphora, inaudible prayers, and an elaborate fraction, but the true meaning and understanding of liturgy eluded

---

[61] Nancy Khalek, *Damascus after the Muslim Conquest: Text and Image in Early Islam* (New York: Oxford University Press, 2011), 43–44.

most of the clergy because they lacked proper education. Interestingly, the modern Syriac liturgy is lacking the Great Entrance, as seen in the Greek liturgy. Bishop Moses Bar Kepha (c.863), in his exposition of Jacobite liturgy, says that there was a "ceremonial procession in which bread and wine are brought out from the sanctuary, carried among the people and brought back to the altar"[62]; however, this disappeared later for various reasons. Baby Varghese has suggested that this happened in part because "the Syrian Orthodox Christians always lived under constraints. Throughout their history, they were a community struggling for survival. Therefore their churches were modest in size and architecture and were often too small for solemn processions, unlike [the] Byzantines." Another reason could be that the Syrian Church always under the persecution and, thus, the liturgy tend adapt to the evolving situations.

As we have seen, the Syriac liturgy was constantly evolving by adapting to the local traditions and cultures, and by enriching itself with other traditions without losing its integrity. As the liturgy has undergone many changes, the Christological position has become more assertive in liturgical expression, as we shall see later in an examination

---

[62]John Dara, *The Commentary of John of Dara on the Eucharist, Moran Etho- 12,* trans. Baby Varghese (Piscataway, NJ: Gorgias Press, 2011), 21.

of the Christology of the Church through a detailed look at the "Fraction Rite."

Further, it is one of the great tragedies of Church history that the Syrian Churches, both East and the West, were separated from the Catholic unity in the fifth and sixth centuries. Even though the ostensible cause for this separation was the controversy over the "two natures" in Christ, as defined in the Council of Chalcedon, the persons who led the factions played a major role in the formulation of the Christology. The East Syrian Church, having Theodore of Mopsuestia as their doctor, followed the teachings of Nestorius and became the "Nestorian Church." The West Syrian Church, following St. Cyril of Alexandria and his successors, then came to be known as the "Monophysite Church." Today, however, it is generally recognized that these divisions existed not so much because of differences in theology, but rather in misunderstandings owing to verbiage, which tragically separated the Churches of Asia and Africa from Byzantium with its Greek culture and Greek imperialism. After its separation from the mainstream Churches, the Syrian Orthodox Church expanded across Asia and developed as a true oriental Christianity. Today, it remains the finest expression of the Christian cultural tradition that is neither Latin nor Greek but belongs to the ancient Semitic world of the Middle East.

Chapter 8: Christology in the Prayers and Liturgies of the Syrian Orthodox Church.

The liturgical prayers and anthems of the Syrian Orthodox Church express its faith and Christology. There is a Latin maxim that addresses the centrality of worship in the life, identity and mission of the Orthodox Church; *"Lex Orandi, Lex Credendi"*. The phrase in Latin literally means the law of prayer ("the way we worship") is the law of belief ("what we believe"). It is sometimes expanded to as, *"lex orandi, lex credendi, lex vivendi"*, further deepening the implications of this truth - how we worship reflects what we believe and determines how we will live. How we worship not only reveals and guards what we believe but guides us in how we live our Christian faith and fulfill our Christian mission in the world by manifesting the continuing presence of the Risen Jesus Christ. Liturgical worship is not an "add on" for the Syrian Orthodox Church. It is the foundation of its identity; expression of what is belief. Worship reveals what truly believe and how the faithful have in relationship to God, one another and the world into which we are sent to carry forward the redemptive mission of Jesus Christ. How the Church worships is a prophetic witness to the truth of what she professes good worship becomes a dynamic means of drawing the entire human community into the fullness of life in Jesus Christ. It attracts - through beauty to Beauty. Liturgical worship informs and transforms both the person and the worshipping community which participates in it. There is reciprocity between worship and life. Pope Pius XII could declare in *Munificentissimus Deus*: "the liturgy of the Church does not engender the Catholic faith, but rather springs from it, in such a way that the practices of the sacred worship proceed from the faith as the fruit comes from the tree ..." (Pius XII. 20). Jesson rightly asserts that "The notion that liturgy supplies normative direction to theology is a methodological principle. To suggest that theology determine the norms for liturgy is a canonical principle" (Jesson 11). This is also very evident in our anthems and our prayers.

In the Early Church, there was liturgical tradition before there was a common creed. These traditions provided the theological framework for establishing the creeds and canons. Christians don't worship because they believe, they believe because the One in whose gift faith lies is regularly met in the common act of worship (Jones 6). Worship is the first articulation of our faith. The series of litanies and petitions in the Syrian Church Eucharist ends with "who" or "to whom" address, "O merciful God who in mercies governs all, we beseech you." These prayers are not making any 'distinctions' of divine and human attributes of God incarnate. According to Ishaq Saka, the purpose of one of the two hymns recited at the Eucharist is "for the confession of One God, the creator of all; that Jesus Christ is one of the Persons of Trinity and after His Incarnation. He is equal to the Father in essence; and that he suffered and died for the redemption of men; making manifest the eternal attributes of the divinity (Saka 75).

The liturgy itself is the attestation of Christological position of the Syrian Orthodox Church. On the preparation for the liturgy, the priest mixes the wine with the water and saying, "O Lord God, mingle this water with this wine, as united your God-head with our humanity" (Kadavil 2003:30). This prayer is a clear allusion for the union of two natures without confusion and separation of two natures. The arrangements of the Sacrificial bread, which is called *furshono* in Syriac, on the altar table is also highlighting the Christology of the Church. If there is only one *furshono* in use, it signifies the Second person in Trinity and showing the union of the divinity and humanity. If two *furshonos* in use, it denotes that "the Son is one in his divinity and humanity." If there are three *furshonos* in use, it indicates the "unity of the divine essence of the three Persons of the Trinity, the Father, the Son and the Holy Spirit. "The Divinity of the Christ in crucifixion not diluted or minimized but remained Christ as full God and full human (Saka 2008:16).

The act of communion is commemoration and redemption. In the Coptic Orthodox liturgy, the priest praying according to St. Basil liturgy at the end part of "fraction and communion".

Amen, Amen, Amen. I believe, I believe, I believe and profess unto my last breath, that

this is the Life-Giving Body, which Your Only Begotten Son, our Lord, God and Savior

Jesus Christ, took of our lady and queen of us all, the Mother of God, the pure Saint

Mary. He made it one with His Divinity without mingling nor interchanging nor

alteration. And declared the proper confession before Pontius Pilate. And gave It up willingly on the Holy Cross on our behalf. I believe that His Divinity never departed from

His Humanity not even for a single instant nor a twinkling of an eye. Given for the

salvation, remission of sins and eternal life to those who partake of them. I believe; I

believe, I believe that this is true. Amen (www.copticchurch.net/).

The bread which is offered is made different elements but formed one sacrificial bread, similarly, according to Dionysius Bar Salibi; "the Son who is from the Godhead was seen with soul and body, in one composite hypostasis and one incarnate nature without confusion and without change and he was offered on the cross as a victim in the flesh for our salvation (Salibi 2011:3-4).

The Christology of the Syrian Orthodox Church is very much expressed in its Liturgy. The order of its Liturgy determines its faith. The Law of Prayers reflected in our ritual format. The origin of our belief is from scriptures, church dogmas and from the apostolic teachings. Liturgy is the place where we profess our faith and liturgy manifests our faith. The way of prayer revealed to us what we pray. When the Church celebrates its sacraments, she confesses her faith from the very beginning starting from the apostles and the liturgy is the constituent element of the Holy Tradition. The belief of the church influences and shapes the liturgy.

Let us look at the Fraction Rite in the Eucharistic Liturgy of the Syrian Orthodox Church and how it expresses its Christological faith through various stages of the fraction.

The Fraction Rite and the Christology of the Syrian Orthodox Church.

During the Christological controversies, the Church began to assert its belief through its liturgical practices, including the Fraction Rite. As will be noted in detail in the subsequent chapters, the most distinctive contribution of the Syriac Orthodox Church to Christological doctrine is its insistence on the oneness of the Person of Christ, which was explained as resulting from the real union of his divinity and humanity (Varghese 2018:13). The expression of the Christology of the Syrian Orthodox Church is in its silent prayers during the time of the fraction rite in the center of the liturgy. The introductory prayer is very significant as the Priest remembers the suffering of Christ in the prayer "Thus truly the Word of God suffered in the flesh. He was slain and broken on the cross: His soul departed His body, but His divinity never left his body or soul… One is Emmanuel and not divided into two natures after the unity, which is indivisible. Thus, we believe, confess and confirm that this body belong to this blood, and this blood belongs to this body" (Saka 2008:88-89). The union, which happened after Christ's death, shows that Immanuel died but His soul returned to his body and rose from the dead. He is One not divided into two natures after the union (Saka 2008:89).

The liturgy of the Syriac Orthodox Church is no exception, as the Christological differences that arose at the Council of Chalcedon emboldened the Syriac Orthodox Church to emphasize its position in its Eucharistic liturgy. In particular, the Fraction Rite in the Syriac Orthodox Church's liturgy was more strongly emphasized; thus, we can view it as an explanation of the Syrian Orthodox Church's understanding of, and faith in, the full divinity and humanity of Christ.

The Christology of the Syrian Orthodox Church very much emphasized in the Fraction Rite- breaking of the bread in the liturgy. Each step in the fraction rite prayer symbolizes the Church's Christology and its faith. The fraction is taking place inside the closed veil on the Altar. The priest lifts up the sacrificial bread and breaks in the middle top portion and it signifies "God the word truly suffered in the flesh and was sacrificed and broken on the cross" (Bar Kepha 1913:67). After setting apart the top portion, the priest breaks the middle of the bottom portion of the bread while holding together the already broken top portion. What this means is "although the Christ's soul was separated from his body, his divinity was in no way separated from his soul or body" (Bar Kepha 1913:67). Another way it is a statement that the divinity and humanity of Christ have equally participated in the salvific action. This is a symbolic expression and belief of the Church that the humanity of Christ joined to the divinity and in fellowship with God's glory through the mediator, the priest (Varghese 2018:46). Further to the fraction, the priest now separates the two parts and holding the upper portion between the fingers of his right hand, he dips it into the chalice while signing the cross with it from east to west and from north to south (Saka 2008:89). This action is directly referring to that "after the soul of the word was separated from his body, the soul returned and was united to his body and the Godhead was not separated either from his body or from his soul at any time. The divinity and humanity are united in One Person, which cannot be separated" (Bar Kepha 1913: 67). This is an example of the fact that "the Syrian Orthodox Church maintained a sound doctrine of the union of divinity and humanity in Christ (Varghese 2018:48). Church Father Bar Salibi explained this step further:

After having signed the body with the blood, he joins the two halves of the bread together, symbolizing that Emmanuel is one, and not divided after the union of the two natures. Again, it shows that after He was sacrificed on the cross, by His blood of the cross, He reconciled and united those who are in heaven with those on earth, and the people with the gentiles and the soul with the body. Then (with the piece that is in his hand), he makes a round on the bread in a circle, indicating that He was sacrificed on the cross for the sins which surrounds the world. Again, making a circle on the bread, the first time from the right side, teaches that He was sacrificed for the sins of the whole world. Then for a second time, from the left to the right indicating that our Lord has restored us from the left to the right indicating that our Lord has restored us from the deeds of the left, that is from error, to the right. As we have said above, the piercing of the half of the bread shows that our Lord was pierced in the flesh. One half placed with (together) with (the other) half indicates that, after He was sacrificed, He united those who are in heaven with those on earth, and soul with body and the people with the gentiles (Bar Salibi 2011 :77-78).

The Eastern Orthodox theologians like Timothy Ware softened their position on the Christology of the non-Chalcedon churches. He recommended and accepted that the theological questions need to be seriously discussed, for the non-Chalcedonian Churches still feel a deep-rooted objection to the Chalcedonian Definition. Nonetheless, of all the "ecumenical" contacts of Orthodoxy, the friendship with the Monophysites seems the most hopeful and the most likely to lead to concrete results in the near future" (Ware 1997:321).

Preparation for the Eucharistic Liturgy:

The priest, in recalling the vision of Isaiah of the holy throne surrounded by angelic forces, invokes an imagery of heaven at the liturgy. The hymns, praises, and worship of the celebrant and faithful provide a sense of their being united to heaven by and in the liturgy. The Passion, Crucifixion, and Resurrection of Jesus are also commemorated through the various steps of the fraction and the commixture of bread and wine. Through each aspect of the Fraction, the participants affirm their faith in the Incarnation, Passion, Crucifixion, and Resurrection of Jesus for God's salvific plan for humankind.

The famous Syriac scholar Ishaq Saka gives us the general pattern of the Syrian Church's liturgy when he writes,

We also remember the heaven and earth, the seas, the sun, the moon, the stars and all the creation both endowed with reason and lacking in reason, angels, archangels, virtues, dominions, principalities, powers, thrones, Cherubim endowed with many different appearances. We also make mention of the Seraphim which Isaiah saw standing around the throne of God and with two wings covering their face, with two wings covering their legs and with two wings flying about saying Holy. We also beg the merciful Lord to send the Holy Spirit upon the gifts which we offer that He might make the Bread the Body of Christ and the Wine the Blood of Christ. But after this spiritual sacrifice is completed, we pray to God for the general peace of the churches, for the right government of the world, for the emperors and for those who are in sickness and affliction. Afterwards, we remember those who have died; the patriarchs, prophets, apostles, and martyrs so that by their prayers, God might receive our prayers. We also pray for the Fathers, Bishops, and all the deceased. Afterwards we say the prayer, which the Savior taught His disciples.[63]

A very important aspect of the Fraction in terms is its emphasis on and assertion of the Church's dogma concerning the relationship of Christ's divinity to his humanity. The Syrian Orthodox Church believes in the essential nature of this relationship as an intrinsic part of God's plan for salvation. As will be discussed, the signs of the Fraction show the divinity and humanity of Christ as participating equally in the salvific action of God.

The Fraction Rite of the Syrian Orthodox Church's liturgy was structured and formulated by the famous scholar Dionysius Bar Salibi (c. 1172). The main source of information about the life and work of Dionysius Bar Salibi is the *Chronicles of the Patriarch Michel, the Syrian*.[64] Dionysius, whose first name was Jacob, was first seen in Syrian history as a deacon who wrote a treatise criticizing the theological position of John of Mardin (c.1165), commonly known as St. Yuhanon of Mardin. Jacob was ordained as a bishop, named Dionysius by Patriarch Michael the Great, and sent to the city of

---

[63] Saka, *Commentary on the Liturgy*, 1–2.

[64] Michael Rabo, *The Syriac Chronicle of Michael Rabo (The Great): A Universal History from the Creation*, trans. by Matti Moosa (Teaneck, NJ: Beth Antioch Press, 2014), 300–302; 559–562.

Amid. Many theological and liturgical works are attributed to Dionysius Bar Salibi, including a long treatise against heresies, a treatise on the Nicene Creed and a confession of faith, and expositions on the Eucharist, Baptism, Myron, and Ordination. Most important of them all is the Order of the Fraction in the Syrian Orthodox Eucharistic liturgy, which is an expression of the Church's faith and belief in the Person of Christ. Most of his treatises are apologetic works against Muslims, Jews, and Crusaders. His explanation of the Syrian Orthodox liturgy, however, was written at the request of Ignatius (c.1140-1184), Bishop of Jerusalem, in order to defend the Syrian Christian faith vis-à-vis Western Crusaders. In his commentary on the Eucharist, Bar Salibi's main sources were the writings of Moses Bar Kepha and the faithful traditions of the Syrian Orthodox Church handed down since the Council of Chalcedon. Dionysius Bar Salibi, in the Introduction to the "Commentary on the Eucharist," explained that his materials are the work of ancient Church Fathers.[65] The commentary begins with a Christological overview

---

[65] Dionysius Bar Salibi, *The Commentary on the Eucharist*, trans. Baby Varghese (Piscataway, NJ: Gorgias Press, 2011), 1-2.

in which Bar Salibi uses a comparison with bread to explain the Church's understanding of its faith:

> …just as the ground wheat is kneaded, and then baked in fire the Son also was united to our feeble flesh without confusion, in the womb of the virgin and by the fire of His divinity. The Son is from the Godhead was seen with soul and body, in one composite hypostasis and one incarnate nature without confusion and (without) change, and he was offered on the cross as a victim in the flesh for our salvation."[66]

Christology in the Fraction Rite:

The Fraction Rite—Overview

The ceremonies of the Fraction, which take place with the curtain closed, are the most complex of all the traditions and rites in the Syrian Orthodox Eucharistic liturgy. They contain many details for breaking and arranging the bread; different patterns, each with a name, are used at different times of the liturgical year. Listed below are the parts of the fraction rite, followed by a detailed examination of each part:

- The curtain is drawn to veil the sanctuary.

---

[66] Ibid., 3.

- The people sing a litany.
- The Fraction Rite:
  - The bread is broken in certain ways.
  - The pieces are dipped in wine.
  - The priest briefly reassembles the pieces.
  - The bread is broken into particles.
- The priest silently prays the Metrical Homily of Jacob of Sarug

Details of the Fraction Rite and their Christology

The curtain is drawn to veil the sanctuary

The curtain is first drawn so that the Fraction can occur in silence. According to Ishaq Saka, the closing of the sanctuary is

…an allusion to the veil which was drawn over the eyes of the heavenly hosts lest they should behold God in the state of His suffering and crucifixion, for they cannot endure beholding their Lord suffer. After the breaking of the bread is done, the veil will be then removed from the faces of the angels and the people, who now become certain that the crucified was Christ.[67]

---

[67] Saka, *Commentary on the Liturgy*, 90-91. "The sanctuary is veiled as a reminder of the time of the redemptive

In addition, according to K. P. Paul, the veiling at the time of fraction represents the torment endured by our Lord on the Cross. The veiling is most significantly connected to the third hour of Jesus' crucifixion at Calvary: "Veiling at the Fraction shows the terror and awe of the moment and mystery of his suffering and death which are signified in the Fraction. It also signifies the Sun setting at the time of crucifixion. The veiling before the procession of the Mysteries represents the Sun becoming dark on the last day."[68] The Fraction embodies the vision of Isaiah in Chapter 6:1-8, as is discussed with reference to one of the litanies used to accompany it below. The priest treats the sacrificial bread as a "live coal," as that which will touch the lips of the

---

passion, death, burial, and resurrection of our Lord, when the earth was engulfed in darkness. (Luke 23:44, 24:1, Matthew 28:1, John 20:1). Mor Severus Mooshé Bar Kepho (c. 813-903) comments that the veil (setoro) is a symbol of the screen which is between us and the hiddenness of heaven as it is said: '...where angels desire to look' (cf. 1 Peter 1:12)." *Order of the Holy* Qurbono *(With Excerpts from the Commentaries of the Holy Fathers)*, rev. (Los Angeles, CA: Syriac Orthodox Resources, 2005), 42, fn. 132, accessed October 16, 2017, http://sor.cua.edu/Liturgy/SvcBook/Service_Book_20080512.pdf

[68] K.P. Paul, *The Eucharist Service of the Syrian Jacobite Church of Malabar* (Piscataway, NJ: Gorgias Press, 2003), 132.

faithful and, by its transforming power, prepare them for the service of God.

As the curtain is drawn across the sanctuary, the celebrant prays an introductory prayer in a low voice while breaking the bread and sprinkling it with wine:

Thus truly the Word of God did suffer in flesh, and was sacrificed and broken on the Cross, and His soul separated from His Body, while His Godhead never separated neither from His Soul nor from His Body. And He was pierced in His side with a spear, and there flowed out of Him blood and water, the atonement of the whole world. And his Body was stained with them. And for the sin of the whole world, the Son died on the Cross, and His Soul came and united with His Body. And He turned us from the work of the left to that of the right. And by the Blood of His Person, He reconciled, united and combined the heavenly with the earthly, the people with the gentiles and the Soul with the Body. And on the third day, He rose from the tomb. One is Emmanuel, and cannot be divided into two natures after the indivisible unity. Thus we believe and thus we confess and thus we confirm that this body belongs to this blood, and this blood belongs to this body.[69]

The prayer begins, "Thus truly the Word of God did suffer in flesh, and was sacrificed and broken on the Cross, and His soul separated from His body, while His Godhead never separated either from His Soul nor from His Body." These words are very much in line with Cyril of Alexandria's understanding of the "one incarnate nature of Christ."[70] This Christology of Cyril is based on St. John 1:14: "The Word became flesh and dwelt among us." Cyril was clear in his position against Eutyches (Monophysite) and Nestorius (dual nature) in emphatically asserting that Christ is One: "Now let the mode of the true Union come in, that so the Word be believed to have been made flesh, i.e. man, and therefore son of David not falsely but as from forth him according to the flesh, having remained too what He was, i.e. God out of God."[71] Cyril thus taught that the hypostatic union of the two natures of the Incarnate Son of God found unity in a single person, Emmanuel, the divine Logos; in addition,

---

[69] Saka, *Commentary on the Liturgy,* 88–89.

[70] St. Cyril of Alexandria, *On the Unity of Christ*, Popular Patristics Series Vol. 13, trans. John Anthony McGuckin (Yonkers, NY: St. Vladimir's Seminary Press, 2012), 35.

[71] Cyril of Alexandria, *That Christ is One*, trans. P. E. Pusey (Ipswich, UK: Oxford, 1881), 298.

the phrase "truly the Word of God did suffer in flesh" points to the humanity of the Logos. For Cyril, the whole mystery of the salvific economy consists of the humbling of the Son of God for our sake, and this kenosis of the Savior further consists of his voluntary submission to human laws. By using the phrase "Incarnated One," Cyril points to the fact that Christ assumes to himself everything that belongs to humanity: birth, growth, hunger, thirst, fatigue, suffering, death and resurrection. As the prayer says, "One is Emmanuel, and cannot be divided into two natures after the indivisible unity"; again, St. Cyril's Christology regarding the conception of two natures is evident in the prayer. For St. Cyril, the two natures are not parallel and independent, but rather, exist in a perfect union which forms "One Incarnate Logos," the "One Emmanuel." So, the above prayer is the expression of the faith of the Church based on the "hypostatic union" of the incarnate Word of God with the man.

This introductory prayer, "He was pierced in His side with a spear, and there flowed out of Him blood and water, the atonement of the whole world," is thus very significant, as the priest also remembers the suffering of Christ on the Cross. Christ suffered in the flesh so that human beings could be reconciled to God. It is an affirmation of the faith of the Church and a rebuke for those who believe in Docetism. The manhood assumed by the Logos was a real manhood. Christ was born of Mary and lived as a full human in this world; His earthly life, passion, and death are real. All these sufferings were real and necessary to our salvation. These teachings are in conjunction with the teachings of St. Cyril that the kenosis of the Jesus Christ is the voluntary submission of human laws and the sufferings on the cross so that salvation is possible.

The People Sing a Litany: The Catholic Hymn During the Fraction

During the Fraction Rite, the faithful sing a hymn as a litany and supplication. This hymn is chosen to suit the season and is called "catholic" because it is general and comprehensive. It was inserted into the Order of the Mass so that the worshippers could sing while the priest is engaged in the Fraction. The purpose of this hymn is to create a solemn atmosphere and to draw the attention of the faithful away from any wandering thoughts. The writings of the early Fathers of the Church, including John of Damascus, used the metaphor of the flaming coal for the Lord's body in the Holy Eucharist as envisioned by Isaiah in Chapter 6, and one of the catholic hymns is based on it:

Seraphim of fire and spirit Isaiah saw in the holy place, each one of them with six wings ministering to Thy divinity. With two, they covered their face to avoid sight of Thy divinity and with two they concealed their feet from being burnt by the Fire. And with two they flew while shouting, "Holy, Holy, Holy art Thou." Holy art Thou, Son of God, bless'd be Thy Honor from Thy place.

Here, the earthly beings are elevated in joining the worship in heaven with the angelic forces as described by Isaiah. The faithful are sacramentally entered into the heavenly sanctuary and joined with the heavenly beings. Purging Isaiah's sinful lips with a coal from the altar helped to burn away the sin and guilt. It is through this purifying and sanctifying 'coal which is the Body of Christ' that we are deified in the Holy Eucharist. When the faithful have received Holy Communion, the Liturgy of St. James refers to "receiving the fiery coal," and the Liturgy of St. John Chrysostom says, "this has touched your lips and has taken away your inequity." Both of these statements directly refer to the sanctification through reception of the Holy Eucharist. The coal in Isaiah's vision points to a substance whose sanctifying power is received through bodily contact. The divinity of God is very much emphasized here and described as worthy of our praise and worship.

Although the celebrant and deacons in the veiled sanctuary of the Syriac Orthodox Church celebrate the Fraction Rite privately, the hymn sung during the rite is an expression that all faithful believers are, in fact, participating with awe and trembling in the Passion of Jesus, which is commemorated through the stages of the Fraction Rite. This is well explained in the *Catechism of the Catholic Church*:

Songs and music fulfill their function as signs in a manner all the more significant when they are "more closely connected ... with the liturgical action," according to three principal criteria: beauty expressive of prayer, the unanimous participation of the assembly at the designated moments, and the solemn character of the celebration. In this way they participate in the purpose of the liturgical words and actions: the glory of God and the sanctification of the faithful.[72]

Through full, conscious, and active participation in the liturgy, believers not only derive spiritual benefits from the liturgy, but they are also elevated to an experience of God's presence and blessing in a profound way through their active interior participation of mind and heart. In this way, the signs and symbols are used to encourage the

---

[72] *Catechism of the Catholic Church* (Liguori, MO: Liguori Publications, 1994), 1157.

congregants' full participation and are designed to incite elevated spiritual feelings. Through active participation in the liturgy, the faithful offer themselves and, in turn, they receive grace from God abundantly. A mystagogical experience of the liturgy through music, signs, and symbols has been part of the liturgical experience from the beginning. Hymns have been traditionally used as medium of expression to praise God and participate in the prayer of the liturgy. Hugh Wybrew, an eminent Orthodox scholar, writes about the importance of signs and symbols in the liturgy, including participation through singing, and says:

[t]he use of the sense of sight in Orthodox worship is only one aspect of the way in which the Liturgy and other services draw the whole person into the prayer of the Church. All the senses and the entire body are involved. In front of the icons people light candles. The invariable use of incense at all services appeals to their sense of smell. Through their hearing music makes its appeal to them, for services are always sung or chanted, never read with the speaking voice. Icons, vestments, and vessels may be touched and kissed; worshippers may be anointed or given blessed bread or other food to eat. They use their bodies as they cross themselves at different

moments in services, and bow or even prostrate themselves at appropriate moments.[73]

The Fracture Proper

The fracture is the ceremonial breaking of the Eucharistic bread. There are various scriptural references to Jesus's breaking of the bread and giving it to his disciples. At the Last Supper, Jesus "broke the bread" (*e.g.*, Matthew 26:26), in an instance generally regarded to be the institution of the Eucharist. The Risen Lord, after walking with two disciples on the road to Emmaus, "broke the bread" with them (Luke 24:30) by which they came to recognize His presence among them; this is often taken by scholars to be a Eucharistic reference. The phrase "breaking the bread" later become a common phrase used to refer to the celebration of the Eucharist. In the scholastic era, St. Thomas Aquinas described the meaning of this rite: "First, it is the breaking of Christ's body in Passion. Secondly, it denotes the various states of the mystical body of Christ, the Church and thirdly, it represents the distribution of graces proceeding from the Christ's passion."[74] The fracture of a single loaf of bread is

---

[73] Hugh Wybrew, *The Orthodox Liturgy: The Development of the Eucharistic Liturgy in the Byzantine Rite* (Crestwood, NY: St. Vladimir's Seminary Press, 1990), 177.

[74] Thomas Aquinas, *Summa Theologiae*, in *Summa Theologica: Complete English Edition in Five Volumes,* col.

mystically important for the Syrian Orthodox Church, as the pieces from the breaking of the single bread are "given to many." St. Paul says, "We are one body, yet many members, all united in Christ" (1 Corinthians 10:17). Similarly, the *Didache* speaks of the gathering around "one bread" as the sign of the gathering into one of the children of God.[75] For these reasons, the Syrian Orthodox Church breaks a single loaf into various particles for the purpose of emphasizing that the one bread in one Eucharist is broken for all, and that those who participate in receiving the Eucharist are in communion with one bishop who represents one God.

Commixture

The mixing of water into wine has a rich symbolic meaning.:

Various symbolic meanings have been attached to this. Some have seen it as a sign of the union of the people with Christ, others of the issues of water and blood from his side on the cross and others again of the union of the two natures in Christ. This latter

---

4, trans. Fathers of the English Dominican Province (Notre Dame, IN: Christian Classics, 1981), ST IIIa, q 83, a.6, ad 6.

[75] Paul Bradshaw, *Search for the Origins of Christian Worship*, 43.

interpretation has led the Armenians to reject the practice because it conflicts with their monophysitism.[76]

The custom of a mixed cup is seemingly as old as the Church itself. Justin Martyr, writing in 150 AD, mentions this practice.[77] Pope Julius (337-352) wrote that the wine and water represent the unity of Christ and the faithful and is a symbol of God's communion with His people.[78] Church Fathers like Clement of Alexandria similarly spoke of the rewards of communion to the faithful who receive the "mixed cup" as "[t]he watered wine, nourishes in faith."[79] For St. Cyprian of Carthage, the "mixed

---

[76] J.G. Davies, ed. "Monophysitism," in *The New Westminster Dictionary of Liturgy and Worship* (Philadelphia: The Westminster Press, 1986), 377.

[77] L.W. Barnard, *Justin Martyr His life and thought* (London: The Cambridge University Press, 1967), 179.

[78] Henry Denzinger, *The Sources of Catholic Dogma*, trans. Roy J. Deferrari (St. Louis: B. Herder Book Co., 1957), at DS 1320.

[79] St. Clement of Alexandria, *The Instructor of the Children*, trans. William Wilson. From Ante-Nicene Fathers, Vol. 2. Ed. Alexander Roberts, James Donaldson, and A. Cleveland Coxe. (Buffalo, NY: Christian Literature Publishing Co., 1885), 2, 2, 19, 4.

cup" is a sign of the communion with the whole Church.[80]

The Syrian Orthodox Church teaches that the mixed chalice represents the two natures of Christ, divine and human.[81] The wine represents his divinity and the water his humanity. Just as the two natures came together in the Incarnation, the divine Logos is present in the Holy Eucharist. As such, the divinity and humanity of Christ are mingled symbolically through the use of wine and water. This action also reminds us that blood and water flowed from our Lord's side when He was pierced on the cross, whereby He bestowed the gift of Spirit (water) and purification from sin (blood) to His Church.

Leavened Bread and its Importance:

The Syrian Orthodox Church uses leavened bread, which is called *lahmo* in Syriac, for the

---

[80] St. Cyprian, *Epistle to Ephesians*, trans. Robert Ernest Wallis. From Ante-Nicene Fathers, Vol.5. ed. Alexander Roberts, James Donaldson, and A. Cleveland Coxe. (Buffalo, NY: Christian Literature Publishing Co., 1886), 62,13.

[81] Moses Bar Kepha and George of the Arabs, *The Book of Life: Two Commentaries on the Jacobite Liturgy,* trans. H.W. Codrington and Richard Hugh Connolly (Oxford: Williams and Norgate, 1913), 35.

celebration of the Eucharist. According to Bar Salibi, "We call it bread (*lahmo*), [because] it is made from leaven, [that is] life. But *patiro* is from dead things, that is from the flour and water alone."[82] It is necessary that the dough be leavened. According to the tradition, leaven was part of the dough used in the Upper Room where the first Eucharist was confected, and a portion of the leaven is kept for the next dough, a practice that continues today. In the making of the *lahmo*, four earthly elements are used: namely flour, olive oil, salt, and water. The fine wheat kneaded with water represents the elements of nature. The olive oil signifies the substance of air. According to Paulose Kadavil, "oil of olive stands for the soul which the Lord united to the human body and [the] making of the *hamiro* is over fire which represents divinity."[83] The pinch of salt represents the Kingdom of God, as our Lord said in Luke 22:19. The importance of salt in the liturgical life of the Old Testament can also be seen in Ezra 6:9 and Leviticus 2:13, and Ezekiel 3:24. The leaven indicates Christ who is Bread of Life. In the Gospels, Our Lord speaks the Kingdom of God as

---

[82] Bar Salibi, *Commentary,* 30.

[83] Poulose Kadavil, *The Eucharist Service of the Jacobite Syrian Christians* (Changanaserry, Kerala, India: Mor Adai Study Center, 2003), 115.

resembling the leaven that a women hid (Mark 13:33). According to Bar Salibi:

The bread of the mysteries is made from flour, symbolizing the element of the earth; from water, symbolizing the element of water; from leaven, symbolizing the air and from salt, symbolizing fire. Bread, that is the body, is made from these four elements. Olive oil symbolizes the soul that our Lord united to Him. Again leaven indicates Christ, faith and the soul.[84]

Bar Hebraeus also connects the leavened bread to the priesthood when he says, "The priest, Melchizedek, offered as a sacrifice leavened bread and wine because the unleavened bread was not used until after the exodus of the children of Israel from Egypt. Thus, our Christian priesthood should offer only leavened bread."[85] The offering of Melchizedek was a shadow of the New Testament Eucharist. As St. Paul says, he was the priest of the Most High God (Hebrews 7:1).

---

[84] Bar Salibi, *Commentary,* 30.

[85] Saka, *Commentary on the Liturgy*, 15.

The Prayer of Breaking and Signing of the Holy Mysteries

The Fraction Rite begins as the Priest stretches out his right hand and makes a sign of cross over the chalice and paten; he draws spiritual energy from the Chalice and Paten with his right hand, turns towards the faithful, and makes the Sign of the Cross over the faithful three times, while saying to the people, "May the mercies of God, our Master and Redeemer Jesus Christ, be with you all." This rite emphasizes the priest's power of blessing. Myron Madden, a Baptist minister who researched the subject of priestly blessings, has noted:

A fundamental point is that the power to bless is be given by the one blessed. It is the character of the ordination. The person who does the blessing is set apart as an instrument for this purpose and the energy conveyed in blessing comes from God, but the authority to exercise this function is bestowed by those who will be its recipients."[86]

This is very much in agreement with the teachings of the Fathers such as Dionysius Bar Salibi[87] that the bread and wine is the spiritual body and blood of

---

[86] Myron C. Madden, *Power to Bless* (New York: Morehouse Publishing, 1999), 26.

[87] Bar Salibi, *Commentary*, 31.

Christ, which is energized by the Holy Spirit, and the priest then transfers these energies to the partakers. These energies are a sanctifying power: "Again the invocation of the Holy Spirit [symbolizes] the mystical union-which is beyond the knowledge-with that sanctifying power which upholds all, [in which] we participate with impassible and immaterial mind."[88] The presence of Christ in the priest's service to the community is explained also in the *Catechism of the Catholic Church*: "In the ecclesial service of the ordained minister, it is Christ himself who is present to his Church as head of His Body, Shepherd of His flock, high priest of the redemptive sacrifice, Teacher of Truth."[89]

The Steps of the Fraction Rite and Their Meaning

Inside the veil, the Priest takes the sacrificial bread in his hands and carries out the following steps in silence:

1. "The priest first lifts up the *furshono* (sacrificial bread) and breaks off the middle of the top portion

---

[88] Bar Salibi, *Commentary,* 69.

[89] *Catechism of the Catholic Church*. (Liguori, MO: Liguori Publications, 1994), 1548.

of the bread."[90] According to Bar Kepha, this signifies that "God the Word truly suffered in the flesh and was sacrificed and broken on the cross."[91]

2. "After setting apart the top portion, the priest breaks the middle of the bottom portion while holding together the broken top portion."[92] This indicates that "although Christ's soul was separated from his body, his divinity was in no way separated from his soul or body."[93] This action also emphasizes "the divinity and humanity of Christ equally participated in the salvific action. As bread and wine are turned into the Body and Blood of Jesus Christ, humanity is joined to the divinity and in fellowship with God's glory through the mediator, the priest. The congregants' participation is also ensured as being part of the unity of Christ's body and each part is shared from a single loaf."[94]

---

[90] Ishaq Saka, *Commentary on the Liturgy*, 89.

[91] Moses Bar Kepha, *Two Commentaries*, 67.

[92] Ishaq Saka, *Commentary on the Liturgy*, 89.

[93] Moses Bar Kepha, *Two Commentaries*, 67.

[94] Ibid., 67.

We Believe in One True God-139

FIG-1: STAGES OF FRACTION

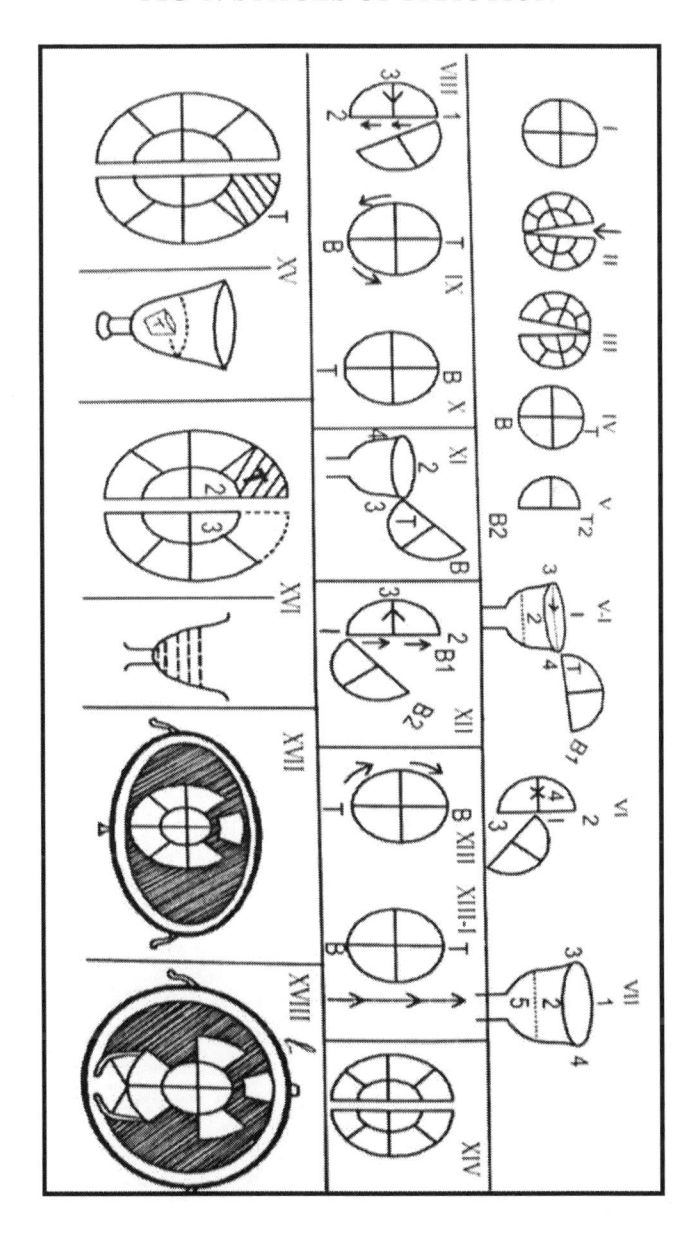

3. "The priest now separates the two parts. Holding the upper portion between the fingers of his right hand, he dips it into the chalice while signing the cross with it from east to west and from north to south."[95] (Diagram V-VIII). By dipping the bread in the wine at this time, the priest evokes the union of Christ's soul with the body. The action refers directly to the fact that "after the soul of the Word was separated from His body, the soul returned and was united to His body, [and] His Godhead [was not] separated either from his body or from His Soul at any time. The Divinity and humanity are united in One Person, which cannot be separated."[96] This description points to the fact that the Syriac Church maintained a sound doctrine of the union of divinity and humanity in Christ. There contains an additional meaning, in that the Incarnation brought the children of sin from the left to the children of righteousness on the right by the death of Jesus on the Cross. Dionysius Bar Salibi offers a detailed explanation of the significance of this action:

> After having signed the body with the blood, he joins the two halves of the bread together, symbolizing that Emmanuel is one, and not divided after the union of the two natures. Again, it shows

---

[95] Saka, *Commentary*, 89.

[96] Moses Bar Kepha, *Two Commentaries*, 67.

that after He was sacrificed on the cross, by His blood of the cross, He reconciled and united those who are in heaven with those on earth, and the people with the gentiles and the soul with the body. Then (with the piece that is in his hand), he makes a round on the bread in a circle, indicating that He was sacrificed on the cross for the sins which surrounds the world. Again, making a circle on the bread, the first time from the right side, teaches that He was sacrificed for the sins of the whole world. Then for a second time, from the left to the right indicating that our Lord has restored us from the left to the right indicating that our Lord has restored us from the deeds of the left, that is from error, to the right. As we have said above, the piercing of the half of the bread shows that our Lord was pierced in the flesh. One half placed with (together) with (the other) half indicates that, after He was sacrificed, He united those who are in heaven with those on earth, and soul with body and the people with the gentiles.[97]

4. "The priest then removes the *furshono* from the chalice and, with it, touches the middle of the second part of the broken bread."[98] At this time, he says, "And He was pierced in His side with a spear, and

---

[97] Bar Salibi, *Commentary*, 77-78.

[98] Saka, *Commentary*, 89.

there flowed out of Him blood and water, the atonement of the whole world. And his Body was stained with them. And for the sin of the whole world, the Son died on the Cross, and His Soul came and united with His Body."[99] This action, in which the priest touches the lower middle portion of the bread with the upper middle portion, is an invocation of what happened on the Cross: the piercing of the side of Christ with a lance. This also reflects that the "Slain One" was besprinkled with his own blood in the Upper Room at the Last Supper when he said, "This is my blood." Furthermore, it signifies the blood and water, which poured out of his side. This transformation is well explained by Moses Bar Kepha:

It is right that we enquire here whether that bread which Christ took and blessed and hallowed and called His body is itself the body which was (taken) from the Virgin, or another beside it: and whether that wine is itself the blood which was (taken) from the Virgin, or other beside it. And we say that it is His body and His blood which was from the Virgin. But perhaps someone will answer and say: How is this possible to be? And we say, even to such a one, that the Right Hand which in the beginning took dust from the earth and changed it and made it the body

---

[99] Ibid.

of Adam, the same has changed this bread and made it the body of the Word, which was from the Virgin; and the same has changed the wine and made it that blood which was from the Virgin. Again, the Holy Spirit which took the flesh of the lamb in Egypt and changed it and made it to be for the redemption of the Hebrews in Egypt, the same has changed this bread and made it that body which was from the holy Virgin, and has changed the wine also and made it that blood which was from the holy Virgin. So understand today also touching the bread and wine which the priest offers: the Holy Spirit who came down into the womb of the Virgin and made that flesh which was from her the body and blood of God the Word, He, the same, comes down upon the altar and makes the bread and wine which are set upon it that body and blood of God the Word which He took from Mary, by the hands of the priest who does the priest's office and offers.[100]

5. "The priest then joins the two parts of the *furshono*. The priest shifts both parts between his fingers from right to left in such a way that top of the wet part, which was between the fingers of his right hand, will now be between the fingers of his left

---

[100] Moses Bar Kepha, *Two Commentaries,* 54.

hand, and vice-versa."[101] This gesture of exchanging the top part to the bottom is intended to signify the coming of Christ to this world from heaven. This action can be understood as a ritual expression of St. Cyril's teaching of *communication of attributes,* wherein properties such as sufferings are attributed to the Incarnated Word in both His divinity and humanity.

6. "The priest dips the lower part, held between the fingers of his right hand, in the chalice and makes the sign of cross in the opposite direction from west to east and from south to north. He takes it out of the chalice and draws a reversed cross."[102] The reversed cross signifies "the death of Christ."[103] It is worth noting here that one part of the *furshono* (bread) should be signed with two crosses, which indicates "salvation is vouchsafed to both Jews and gentiles."[104] Only one cross should be signed on the second part, signifying "salvation for those who have departed from this world."[105] Now, the priest

---

[101] Saka, *Commentary*, 89.

[102] Saka, *Commentary*, 89.

[103] Ibid., 89.

[104] Bar Salibi, *Commentary*, 78.

[105] Ibid.

We Believe in One True God-145

has signed three crosses on the Body and three on the Blood. Then, he joins the two parts to demonstrate "the return of Christ's soul to be united with his body."[106] The union, which happened after Christ's death, shows that "Immanuel died, but His soul returned to His body and rose from the dead."[107] He is one and not divided into two natures after the union. The blood signifies the soul; as Scripture says, "the soul of every being is his blood" (Leviticus 17:11). Moses Bar Kepha explains the faith of the Syrian Orthodox Church regarding this action and belief in the following way:

> Again, where as he brings some of the blood and signs the body, he makes a union of the soul with the body; and he shews that after the soul of the Word was separated from His body, His soul returned and was united to His body; howbeit His Godhead was in no wise separated either from His body or from His soul, neither can it be separated. And that bread is the body of the God the Word, but the wine is His soul; for the blood is a symbol of the soul, as it is written: "The Soul of all flesh is the blood". But again, whereas, after he has signed (with) some of the blood over the

---

[106] Ibid.

[107] Bar Kepha, *Two Commentaries,* 66.

body, he unites and fits together these two halves of the *perista* one with another, he symbolizes and shews by this that Emmanuel is one, and is not divided into two natures after the union.[108]

In the above quotation, Moses Bar Kepha explains what the priest does in light of its Christological importance. The priest dips the one half into the chalice and brings it back over to the other half of the bread to sprinkle over it, first over the five holes on the bread and then on the broken part of the bread. This is an allusion to a "union of the soul with the body." Here, the blood and the body are joined together, emphasizing that "His Godhead was not separated from the flesh." Then the priest puts together the two halves, which symbolizes that "Emmanuel is One and cannot be divided into two natures".

7. "The priest then moves the two joined parts of the sacrificial bread back to their original positions, from left to right facing up."[109] Bar Salibi says, "This is a reminder of the coming down of Christ to earth

---

[108] Ibid., 66.

[109] Saka, *Commentary*, 89.

and the transference of the faithful from darkness to light and truth."[110]

When the broken halves are next dipped into the chalice, there is an explicit mention of the pierced body sprinkled with blood. The prayer which accompanies this action says, "You are the Christ God, who was pierced by a lance in His side on the heights of Golgotha in Jerusalem for our sake. You are the lamb of the God who took away the sins of the world and redeemed it."[111]

8. "The priest, bowing, elevates the two joined parts of the bread over his head, and "priest waves them from left to right"[112] as he says, "He is risen," to show that Christ brought us back from error to truth. The left stands for the condemnation and darkness, while the right is for those saved in Christ; they are in the light (St. Mathew 25:33). This action also recalls the Sign of the Cross made by the faithful in which the movement from the left shoulder to the right stands for Jesus' descent into hell (the left side) and his movement to heaven (the right side). When the two halves are put together and the priest raises

---

[110] Bar Salibi, *The Commentary,* 79.

[111] Saka, *Commentary,* 91.

[112] Ibid., 89.

them above his head, this is an explicit identification of Christ's resurrection. The above immersion and rising of the bread from the chalice emphasizes the imitation of his Passion, communion with Christ, and the sharing of his cross. Meantime, the fans are waved as an indication of the quake which happened at His resurrection. Ishaq Saka explains this as follows:

The union, which happened after Christ' death, shows that Immanuel died, but His soul returned to His body and rose from the dead. He is one and not divided into two natures after the union. The priest, bowing, elevates the two joined parts of the bread over his head, and waves them in a circular manner from right to left in an allusion to the death of Christ for the world. Again, he waves them from left to right to show that Christ brought us back from error to truth, as he says, "He is risen."[113]

9. "The priest brings down the two parts of the *furshono*. He puts the right part over the left. He presses them with two fingers of his left hand." [114] The Priest says the following prayer during this time: "And by the blood of his Person, He

---

[113] Saka, *Commentary*, 90.

[114] Ibid., 89.

reconciled, united and combined the heavenly with the earthly, the people with the gentiles and the Soul with the Body." [115]These gestures allude to the fact that "after Christ's death God has united the heavenly hosts with the people on earth and the Jews with gentiles."[116]

10. "The priest then separates the upper particles of the right part and puts it in the chalice, saying, 'This body is of this blood, and this blood is of this body.'"[117] With these words, he signifies that the particles are the one Body of the Incarnate Word of God. At the Last Supper Jesus said, "This is my Body, This is my Blood," (Matt 26:28). The Syrian Orthodox Church believes and confess that the Holy Spirit descended onto the Holy Eucharist and transubstantiated the bread and wine into the blood and body of Jesus Christ. As such, this is the real presence of Christ and His Body, and the Church does not use the term 'real presence' in any sort of figurative way.

---

[115] Syriac Orthodox Church Trilingual Eucharist Service book, ed. Kuriakose Corepiscopa Moolayil (Kottayam, Kerala: Mor Adai Study Centre), 147.

[116] Bar Kepha, *Two Commentaries*, 68.

[117] Saka, *Commentary,* 90.

Here, we should note St. Cyril's statements on the Eucharist as the Body of Christ. For St. Cyril, a close connection exists between the Body of Christ and the incarnation of the Word, which is the union between a human nature and the divine Logos. In order to refute the teachings of the Nestorius, according to St. Cyril, "the Body of Christ is that of a man 'sanctified and deified' through its union with the Word."[118] One of the distinctive elements of St. Cyril's Christology is the way in which he conceives of the union of two natures in the person of Jesus. For St. Cyril, the two natures are not parallel and independent, but in so perfect a union that they make one single nature or a single Logos. St. Cyril further demonstrates the close connection that exists between the Eucharistic body and Incarnation of the Word. The Eucharistic body is the same human-divine presence as in the Incarnation of Logos. In order to repudiate the position of the Nestorius, St. Cyril emphasized that the Eucharistic body has power to give life. The Eucharistic Body aims to transform our life and enables us to achieve communion with Christ. Through these teachings, St. Cyril helps us to understand that the union, which is realized between believers and Christ in the Eucharist, is analogous to the hypostatic union.

---

[118] Cyril of Alexandria, *That Christ is One,* 267.

11. "The priest then separates the particle of the second part and dips it into the chalice. With it, he touches, first, the part from which it was detached and then the other part."[119] Here, he shows that the Blood signifies the soul that returned to and united with the Body after Christ's resurrection. As well, the fraction may be regarded as parallel to the Incarnation. Moses Bar Kepha explains:

> Again, we say thus: just as in the case of the holy Virgin Mary the Father willed that the Son should be incarnate, but the Son came down into the womb of the Virgin and became incarnate, and the Spirit also came down to the Virgin and caused the Son to be incarnate of her: so here also in the case of the altar: the Father wills that the Son be united hypostatically to the bread and wine, and that they become His body and His blood; but the Son comes down that He may be hypostatically united to them; and the Spirit also comes down that He may unite them to Him, even as He caused Him to be incarnate of the Virgin.[120]

---

[119] Saka, *Commentary*, 90.

[120] Bar Kepha and George of the Arabs, The *Book of Life,* 60.

Here, Moses Bar Kepha denotes the direct relationship between the Incarnation and the sprinkling of the blood on the broken body of the Eucharist. The priest picks up the top particle (#8, see diagram) and immerses it in the blood of the chalice, then brings it back to touch on the detached portion from which particle #8 was detached. This is an allusion to the soul, which is returned to the Body of Christ after the resurrection. Bar Kepha connects this action to the Incarnation of Christ, as the second Person in the Trinity came to the womb of the Virgin and was united with humanity by the power of the Holy Spirit. Similarly, on the table of Altar, it is the will of the Father that the Son unite the appearances of bread and wine with His Body and the Blood by the presence of the Holy Spirit. Moses bar Kepha thus draws a parallel between the fraction and the Incarnation to highlight the hypostatic union of the divinity and humanity of Christ.

12. "The priest then places the piece on the paten, as well as the other two parts that were between the fingers of the left hand."[121] After this, the priest breaks and arranges the bread in any of the three patterns of arrangement, according to the liturgical seasons as follows:

---

[121] Saka, *Commentary*, 90.

a. Lamb (Emro) Pattern: This arrangement is done from the first Sunday of the Church calendar (*Koodosh-Eto*) until the Saturday before Easter. This is the simplest form of arrangement and is accomplished by dipping piece #8 into the chalice and sprinkling the pieces on the paten in the following order:

FIG.2: LAMB PATTERN ARRANGEMENT

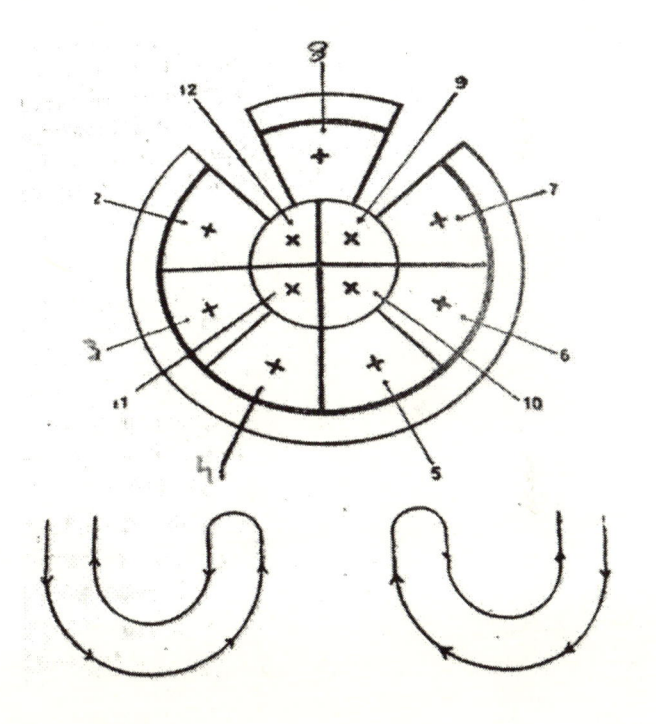

First two times 2,3,4,5,6,7,9,10,11,12.

Third time 7,6,5,4,3,2,12,11,10,9

FIG.3: HUMAN PATTERN ARRANGEMENT

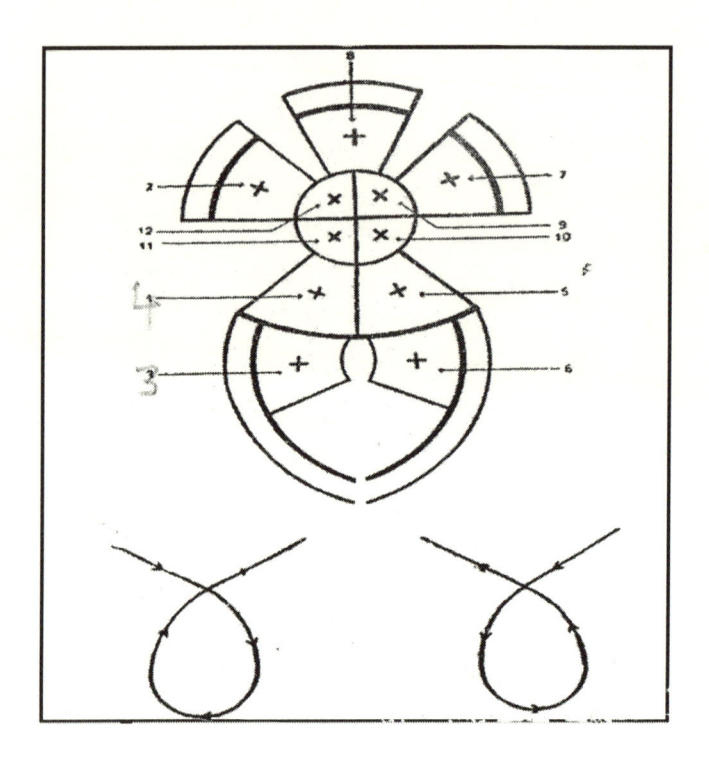

b. Human (Barnosho) Pattern: This arrangement is done from the Easter Sunday until the Feast of the Holy Cross (September 14).

Here, the priest dips piece #8 into the chalice and sprinkles the pieces on the paten in the following order:

First two times: 2,12,10,5,6,3,4,11,9,7.

Third time: 7,9,11,4,3,6,5,10,12,2.

We Believe in One True God-155

c. Crucifix (Sleebo) Pattern: This arrangement is done from the Feast of the Cross until the First Sunday of the Church calendar (Koodos-Etho).

FIG.4: CRICIFIX PATTERN ARRANGEMENT

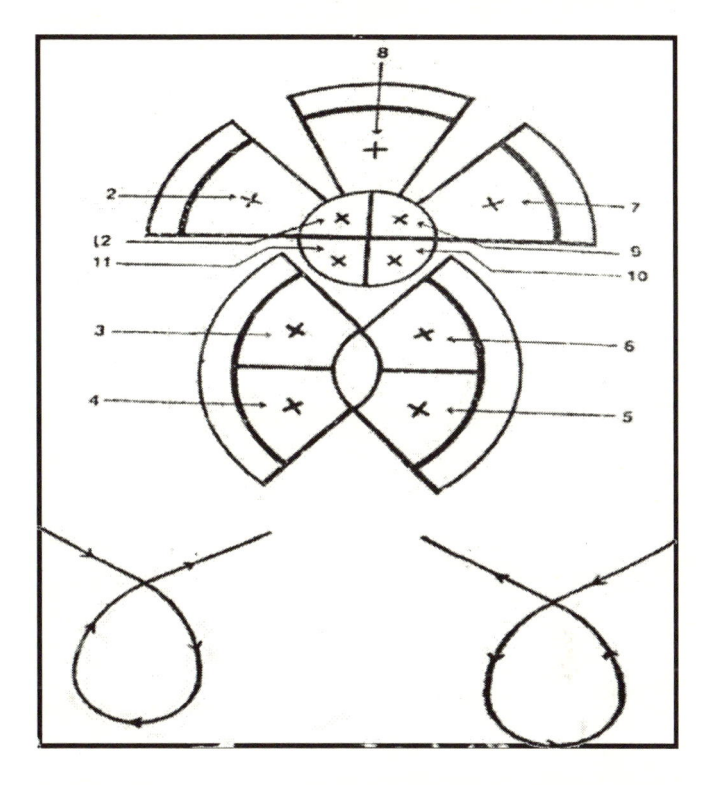

Piece #8 is dipped into the chalice and sprinkled on the pieces on the paten in the following way:

First two times: 2,12,10,6,5,4,3,11,9,7.

Third time: 7,9,11,3,4,5,6,10,12,2

Each of these patterns is associated with the liturgical calendar of the Syriac Orthodox Church. The liturgical calendar year begins with *qudosh 'idto*, the Consecration of the Church, which falls on the eighth Sunday before Christmas. The liturgical year of the Church is divided into seven cycles based on the six feasts which are Christmas on December 25th, Epiphany on January 6th, Easter on the first Sunday after the first full moon following the vernal equinox (variable dates), Transfiguration on August 6th, Assumption of Mother of God on August 15th and the Feast of the Holy Cross on September 14th. The Lamb pattern is the representation of Jesus, the Lamb of God, who experienced the events of the Paschal Mystery from the Maundy Thursday until the Saturday before Easter. The *Barnosho* (Human) pattern is the representation of the resurrected God in his human and divine divine natures. This pattern continues until the Feast of the Cross (September 14th). The Cross pattern begins on September 14th, and all the scripture readings are arranged for the veneration of the Cross.

The three seasons are arranged in such way that the prayers of the corresponding season highlight the feast and events of the season. For example, during the "Lamb" season, the theme of the prayers emphasize the sanctification and dedication of the faithful, the purpose of Incarnation, the Revelation of the Holy Trinity at Epiphany, and the remembrance of the departed clergies and faithful. The Prefatory prayer (Promeon) and the Common prayer (*Sedro*) also speak to the events associated with the seasons. The purpose of the arrangements of such prayers is to glorify and understand the mystery of Christ from His Incarnation to His Ascension. It also provides a way for the faithful to mark the important events in the liturgical life of the church. That is, the readings and prayers are arranged in such way that the faithful can live a life in sanctity and according to the teachings and faith of the Church.

The Metrical Homily of Jacob of Serug Recited During the Fraction

The priest, holding the paten on his left hand and resting his right hand over the top of the bread, prays from a text which seeks forgiveness from God the Father for the sins of the celebrant and the partakers of this Eucharist on behalf of the Son who was sacrificed for the world on the Cross. The metrical homily of St. Jacob Serug (A.D. 451–521), which is sung by the priest in silence during this time of the fraction, provides an early indication of the Church's understanding of salvation. The priest who recites the homily in silence contemplates Christ's Passion on the Cross. The homily begins by alluding to the suffering of our Lord Jesus Christ and then speaks of the sinful nature of mankind:

O Father who is Truth, this is your Son offered as a sacrifice that pleases you. Receive Him since He died for me and vouchsafed my forgiveness. Accept this sacrifice from my hands and be pleased with me. Do not remember the sins I committed against your Lordship; His blood, which sinful men shed on Golgotha, pleads for me. So, accept my petition for His honor. How manifold are my sins and how great are your mercies! If you weighed my sins, your compassion would surpass the heavy load of the mountains in the balance. Contemplate my sins and consider the sacrifice offered on their behalf. No doubt, immolation and sacrifice are much greater than sins. For my sins, your beloved Son, suffered the nails and the lance. There is in His suffering what please you and saves me. Praise to the Father who delivered His Son for our redemption, and adoration to the Son who died on the Cross and offered life to all of us. Praise to the Holy Spirit who began and consummated the mystery of our salvation. O Trinity, exalted above all, have mercy on us all.[122]

---

[122] Kadavil, *The Eucharist Service*, 124–5.

The work of Jacob of Serug reflects the Christological position of the Syrian Orthodox Church in and around Edessa. The "Divine Economy" is the main theme in the work of Jacob of Sarug, as indicated in *Salvation in Christ According to Jacob of Sarug*, by Thomas Kollamparampil:

Hence Christ stands as the key to the understanding as well as the realization of the whole economy of salvation. For Jacob the understanding of divine realities is not merely a cerebral process but primarily a personal and participative knowledge of the revealed realities. Such revealed realities invite the whole humanity to respond to the divine initiative as well as encourage all to partake of the divine bliss through incarnate Son. This participation in divine bliss is made concrete in a sacramental manner, especially, in the liturgical celebrations.[123]

The priest sings the *memre* in silence because Jacob of Sarug presents "the mystery of Christ through his symbolic-typological vision that culminates in mystical silence. According to him, in silence, away

---

[123] Thomas Kollamparampil, *Salvation in Christ According to Jacob of Serug* (New Jersey: Gorgias Press, 2010), 4.

from worldly chaos, the spirit inspires the faithful with the knowledge of the Truth."[124]

The prayer concludes the *memre* with the invocation of the Holy Trinity, which expresses Jacob of Sarug's idea of the economy of the Trinity. Jacob of Sarug believes that the "Father in collaboration with the Son created the world and the divinity inhabits in the world as the intellect inhabits in a man. Moreover, the Son came to inhabit our flesh...and the Spirit sanctifies and perfects the world."[125]

The *memre* of Jacob of Sarug thus highlights the position of the Syriac Orthodox Church that the divinity of Christ is manifested in creation, redemption, and salvation. In this way, the whole history of salvation consists of the divine initiative with a human response, and Christ is the actualization of the engagement between divine mercy and humanity. Jacob of Sarug uses the Cyrillian Christology to defend the unity of Christ and Christ-centered salvation. The divinity of Christ is manifested through the sacrifice on the Cross, which brings humanity closer to the Trinity. The mystery of the Incarnation of God, together with the

---

[124] Kollamparampil, *Salvation in Christ*, 29.

[125] Ibid., 61.

mystery of the Holy Trinity, is the theme of the *memre*. The Second Person of the Trinity accepted the incarnate state for the dispensation of salvation.

The Catholic (General) Hymn:

The hymn sung by the faithful during the Fraction is called 'catholic' because it is general and comprehensive. The hymn is chosen in order to suit the season of the celebration of the Eucharist. It is inserted into the Mass so that the worshippers can experience the nature and mighty acts of God through song. It is intended to lead the faithful to penitence, thanksgiving, adoration, love, and fear of God.

One of the two most common hymns sung by the faithful is the hymn "The angels as seen by Isaiah." With the eye of the Spirit, Isaiah saw God Incarnate in a human form seated on the throne, high and exalted, and the train of his robe filled the temple. This kind of heavenly atmosphere described in the hymn reminds the faithful of the presence of God in their midst.

According to Ishaq Saka, the hymn recited at the time of the fraction also emphasizes the Christology of the Syrian Orthodox Church:

The purpose of one of the two hymns recited at the Eucharist is for the confession of One God, the creator of all; that Jesus Christ is one of the Persons of Trinity and after His Incarnation, He is equal to the Father in essence; and that he suffered and died for the redemption of men; making manifest the eternal attributes of the divinity.[126]

Breaking of the Bread into Particles:

The celebrant then tinctures the Body with the Blood and says the following prayer silently:

> You are Christ God who was pierced in His side on the heights of Golgotha in Jerusalem for us. You are the Lamb of God Who takes away the sins of the world and saves it. You pardon our offenses, forgive our sins and make us to stand at your right-hand side.[127]

During the recitation of this prayer, the priest begins to break the consecrated bread into particles, each called *gmurto*, which means "live coal." As noted earlier, this is an allusion to Isaiah 6:6. The priest then arranges them in the form of a crucified person

---

[126] Saka, *Commentary on the Liturgy*, 75.

[127] Syriac Orthodox Church Trilingual Eucharist Service book, ed. Kuriakose Corepiscopa Moolayil (Kottayam, Kerala: Mor Adai Study Centre), 148.

or a lamb. He puts one *gmurto* on top, separate from the others, in order to signify the head of the crucified Christ.

According to the rubrics of the St. James liturgy, the priest performs the following steps during the breaking of the particles.

The priest lifts up the paten with his left hand and draws it close to the chalice. He takes the *gmurto* with the fingers of his right hand and dips it into the Blood. He signs the cross over all the particles without leaving one particle not sprinkled with the Blood. He does this in allusion to the soul of Christ, which departed his body and then returned and was united with it. When he calls the Lamb of God and beseeches Him to forgive the sins of the world and set the faithful up at His right hand, the priest repeats what he has already performed in allusion to the slain Lamb being sprinkled with the blood. When the broken halves are dipped into the chalice, it is an explicit mention of the pierced body sprinkled with blood. When the two halves are put together and raised overhead by the priest, it is an explicit identification of Christ's resurrection. It is an emphasis on the imitation of the passion, communion with Christ and sharing His cross.[128]

The breaking of the bread shows the oneness of the believers who partake of the one bread, which is Christ, though they are many believers. Each piece is considered to be a full and complete presentation of the Body of Christ. The Syrian Orthodox liturgy speaks of the following understanding in the treatment of these individual pieces:

Again, in breaking the body into many coals, after he [priest] has cast the coal of the body into the blood, in this also he [priest] does as our Lord did, who broke His body and divided it to His disciples in the upper chamber. Again, he breaks it into many coals, that it may suffice for all the faithful who are present. And it behooves all intelligent and discerning priests that when they cause the faithful to partake of the body of our Lord, whether they be boys who partake, or men, or girls, or women, they break not one of the coals into two or three, but give each coal entire to one (man) or to one (woman); that thus the cross may be given whole on each coal to each one of the receivers, and the figure of the cross

---

[128] Saka, *Commentary on the Liturgy*, 91–92.

which is on the coal may not be defaced by breaking the coal.[129]

Each particle of the bread is the full representation of the whole loaf. The Church teaches that even receiving a small piece by the faithful is receiving the entire body of Christ. The Christological importance of the full loaf is well explained by Bar Salibi. Bar Salibi connects the single loaf with the Christology of St. Cyril when he says:

The chosen bread (*presto*), that is the stamped bread of the mysteries, is made from (different) elements set apart for the liturgy and the sacramental offering. Similarly, the Son who is from the Godhead was seen with soul and body, in one composite hypostasis and one incarnate nature without confusion and (without) change and he was offered on the cross as a victim in the flesh for our salvation.[130]

---

[129] George of the Arabs, *The Book of Life,* 68–69.

[130] Baby Varghese, *The Commentary of Dionysius Bar Salibi*, 3–4.

Summary

In this chapter, we have seen that the breaking of the bread during the Eucharistic liturgy symbolizes the crucifixion and death of our Lord on the cross. The various parts of the liturgy proclaim Christ as divine—for example, the allusions to the passage from Isaiah 6 clearly point to the Son of God as a member of the Divine Trinity. In particular, the hymn recited by the faithful during the time of fraction describes how the heavenly hosts worship the Lord God. The hymn presents the liturgy as a sanctification of time and space whereby heaven and earth are reconciled around the "table of life," where we share in the Lord's Supper and proclaim together with all creation our Lord's resurrection until He comes again.

In its many and detailed parts, the Fraction Rite also shows that the Word suffered truly in the flesh, which is the cornerstone of faith in the Syrian Orthodox Church. As the priest signs the Body with the Blood, he signifies that Christ was pierced on the side with a lance. When the priest breaks the bread and sprinkles it with the Precious Blood, this is a reminder that the body and soul of Christ, which were separated in death, were reunited at the resurrection. The separation of the sacrificial bread, shown by holding the top and bottom portions simultaneously, emphasizes that although the soul of

Christ was separated from the body, His divinity was not separated from the soul or the body. After having signed the sacrificial bread with the cross, the priest "joins the two halves together, symbolizing that Emmanuel is one, and not divided after the union of two natures."[131] The broken halves held together and being lifted up over the head signifies the Resurrection of our Lord. The priest, by dipping a piece of the broken bread into the chalice and signing the body in the form of a cross, symbolically brings forth the union of the soul with the body. The one piece of the coal in the chalice is a reminder of the unification of Christ's divinity and humanity. The chalice is a mixture of wine and water, which symbolizes Christ's divinity and humanity. Adding a piece of the coal, which is the resurrected body, signifies that these three aspects of Christ -divinity, soul and the resurrected body- are united together. The Cyrilian understanding of the hypostatic union is well explained in this action by Moses Bar Kepha:

Whereas he takes some of the body and dips it in the blood, and brings some of it (the blood) and signs over the body, he shews that this Slain One was besprinkled with His blood in the upper room when He said, "This is my blood", and on the

---

[131] Bar Salibi, *The Commentary*, 77.

cross when His side was pierced with a spear and there came forth from it blood and water, and He was besprinkled therewith. Again, whereas he brings some of the blood and signs the body, he makes a union of the soul with the body: and he shews that after the soul of the Word was separated from His body, His soul returned and was united to His body: howbeit His Godhead was in no wise separated either from His body or from His soul, neither can it be separated.[132]

Here, Moses Bar Kepha gives an analogy of the union of soul and body with the union of divinity and humanity of Christ. This is also a reflection of the Athanasian Creed, which says, "For as the reasonable soul and flesh is one man, so God and man is one Christ."[133] Bar Salibi agrees with this approach, noting, "After the soul had separated from the body of the Word, His soul again is united with His body, or from His soul, and it will not be separated."[134]

In the Fraction Rite, it is clear that the Syrian Orthodox Church follows the Cyrilian explanation of the Nature of Christ. These actions affirm that the

---

[132] Moses Bar Kepha, *Two Commentaries*, 67.

[133] Athanasius, *On the Incarnation*, 37.

[134] Bar Salibi, *The Commentary*, 77.

bread and wine, which become the life-giving Body of Christ, have the same human-divine presence as the historic body of the Christ, and this is parallel to the Eucharistic doctrine of St. Cyril of Alexandria. For St. Cyril, the hypostatic union expresses that the incarnate Word of God is a unique subject, at the same time God and man, and one single person. St. Cyril argues that the Eucharistic body has the power to make present the true Body of Christ. The faithful who receive the Eucharistic body of Christ are thus brought into communion with Christ, which is analogous to the hypostatic union of the Incarnate Logos. The Eucharistic body has the same human-divine presence as the historic body of Christ, and the Syrian Orthodox Church, in this way, symbolically teaches the doctrine of the hypostatic union of the Incarnate Logos as described by St. Cyril of Alexandria.

Chapter. 9: Christology Today:

During the Christological controversies, the Church began to assert its belief through its liturgical practices, including the Fraction Rite. As will be noted in detail in the subsequent chapters, the most distinctive contribution of the Syriac Orthodox Church to Christological doctrine is its insistence on the oneness of the Person of Christ, which was explained as resulting from the real union of his divinity and humanity (Varghese 2018:13). The expression of the Christology of the Syrian Orthodox Church is in its silent prayers during the time of the fraction rite in the center of the liturgy. The introductory prayer is very significant as the Priest remembers the suffering of Christ in the prayer "Thus truly the Word of God suffered in the flesh. He was slain and broken on the cross: His soul departed His body, but His divinity never left his body or soul… One is Emmanuel and not divided into two natures after the unity, which is indivisible. Thus, we believe, confess and confirm that this body belong to this blood, and this blood belongs to this body" (Saka 2008:88-89). The union, which happened after Christ's death, shows that Immanuel died but His soul returned to his body and rose from the dead. He is One not divided into two natures after the union (Saka 2008:89).

The liturgy of the Syriac Orthodox Church is no exception, as the Christological differences that arose at the Council of Chalcedon emboldened the Syriac Orthodox Church to emphasize its position in its Eucharistic liturgy. In particular, the Fraction Rite in the Syriac Orthodox Church's liturgy was more strongly emphasized; thus, we can view it as an explanation of the Syrian Orthodox Church's understanding of, and faith in, the full divinity and humanity of Christ.

The Christology of the Syrian Orthodox Church very much emphasized in the Fraction Rite- breaking of the bread in the liturgy. Each step in the fraction rite prayer symbolizes the Church's Christology and its faith. The fraction is taking place inside the closed veil on the Altar. The priest lifts up the sacrificial bread and breaks in the middle top portion and it signifies "God the word truly suffered in the flesh and was sacrificed and broken on the cross" (Bar Kepha 1913:67). After setting apart the top portion, the priest breaks the middle of the bottom portion of the bread while holding together the already broken top portion. What this means is "although the Christ's soul was separated from his body, his divinity was in no way separated from his soul or body" (Bar Kepha 1913:67). Another way it is a statement that the divinity and humanity of Christ have equally participated in the salvific action. This is a symbolic expression and belief of the Church that the humanity of Christ joined to the divinity and in fellowship with God's glory through the mediator, the priest (Varghese 2018:46). Further to the fraction, the priest now separates the two parts and holding the upper portion between the fingers of his right hand, he dips it into the chalice while signing the cross with it from east to west and from north to south (Saka 2008:89). This action is directly referring to that "after the soul of the word was separated from his body, the soul returned and was united to his body and the Godhead was not separated either from his body or from his soul at any time. The divinity and humanity are united in One Person, which cannot be separated" (Bar Kepha 1913: 67). This is an example of the fact that "the Syrian Orthodox Church maintained a sound doctrine of the union of divinity and humanity in Christ (Varghese 2018:48). Church Father Bar Salibi explained this step further:

> After having signed the body with the blood, he joins the two halves of the bread together, symbolizing that Emmanuel is one, and not divided after the union of the two natures. Again, it shows that after He was sacrificed on the cross, by His blood of the cross, He

reconciled and united those who are in heaven with those on earth, and the people with the gentiles and the soul with the body. Then (with the piece that is in his hand), he makes a round on the bread in a circle, indicating that He was sacrificed on the cross for the sins which surrounds the world. Again, making a circle on the bread, the first time from the right side, teaches that He was sacrificed for the sins of the whole world. Then for a second time, from the left to the right indicating that our Lord has restored us from the left to the right indicating that our Lord has restored us from the deeds of the left, that is from error, to the right. As we have said above, the piercing of the half of the bread shows that our Lord was pierced in the flesh. One half placed with (together) with (the other) half indicates that, after He was sacrificed, He united those who are in heaven with those on earth, and soul with body and the people with the gentiles (Bar Salibi 2011 :77-78).

The Eastern Orthodox theologians like Timothy Ware softened their position on the Christology of the non-Chalcedon churches. He recommended and accepted that the theological questions need to be seriously discussed, for the non-Chalcedonian

Churches still feel a deep-rooted objection to the Chalcedonian Definition. Nonetheless, of all the "ecumenical" contacts of Orthodoxy, the friendship with the Monophysites seems the most hopeful and the most likely to lead to concrete results in the near future" (Ware 1997:321).

Christology in the daily life off the Syrian Orthodox Church faithful:

The Syrian Orthodox Christians in the Middle East wore a special band from the feast of the Annunciation (March 25th) until the Easter. The band is called "Siboro" means "good news'. It is the good news given to Mary about the divine God coming to the human world. The band consists of one white thread and one red thread wounded together as one thread with distinctive colors of white and red. The white thread symbolizes the divine nature and purity of Christ and the red thread symbolizes the human nature. The red and white threads are wounded together and is a representation of divine nature uniting with the human nature through Mary. On the day of the Annunciation, the Divine Christ joined with the humanity and formed one union (one thread). This denotes that two natures of Christ made hypostatic union at the womb of Mary and not lost its divinity or humanity at the union. The faithful wear it as a waistband, as necklace or tie on the sacramental bread, to decorate the Holy altar during the period of Annunciation and the Easter. This is an emphasis of the faith and Christology of the faithful in their spiritual life and an attestation of the Christology of the Syrian Orthodox Church. (www.Syriacpress.com /Suboro-Siboro).

The Syrian Orthodox Church used signs and symbols in the prayers and the liturgies. Also, there are inscriptions on churches and crosses to highlight the Christological position of the church. The adoption of fifth century crosses by the Church which is commonly known as Ankh crosses and has an inscription on it "One God" with the first three letters for Jesus (Longenecker 2015:139). Presenting Jesus as "One God" with divine and human natures is very explicit in all aspects of church life.

The liturgical prayers addressed to the Father, the First Person in the Trinity, because the celebrant, the Priest, is representing the Christ in the Eucharist; as such he is a mediator between the God the Father and the faithful. Strictly speaking, the 'exchange of predicates' between the Divine and human nature of Christ in the Eucharist is not often used except in few places where the incarnation is highlighted (Varghese 2018:9). In its theology and liturgy, the Syrian Orthodox Church always emphasized equally the divinity as well as humanity of Christ. A prayer of Severus of Antioch used by the Coptic Church today in the Troparion says "O Only Begotten Son and the Word of God the immortal and everlasting, accepting everything for our salvation, the Incarnated from the Theotokos ever-Virgin Saint Mary, without change, Christ God becoming Man, crucified, through death treating death, one of the Holy Trinity to whom is glorification with the Father and the Holy Spirit, Save us" (Youssef 2004:139-148). The union of divine and human natures intrinsically redemptive as seen in the prayers of Severus of Antioch.

The Syrian Orthodox Church and its Christology went through so many rejections and oppressions as noted by an Episcopalian Church scholar "It is within the possibilities of Gods providence that they might yet take new root downwards and bear fruit upwards, if the people who still cling passionately to their ancient faith, were once freed from the domination of foreign religion and power, under which they have so long and so cruelly been oppressed. As it is, in all their present feebleness, they are the representatives of the ancient church, which once flourished in these eastern and southern lands" (Cults 1890:446).

The Syrian Orthodox Church withstood the heavy blows of Byzantine persecution and maintained the apostolic faith, affirmed by the three ecumenical councils. The Holy See of Antioch remained united with the See of Alexandria, and they continue in communion with the Armenian Orthodox Church and the Ethiopian Church sharing the same faith and doctrine.

The term 'Monophysites' used to call the non-chalcedonian churches is "comparatively a modern term" (Samuel 2001:22f). The Western theologians thought that using "Monophysites" is of convenience and sufficient enough because the non-Caledonian churches adhere to "one incarnate nature". The "Eutychianism" or "Monophysitism" is a distorted version of the Christology of the Syrian Orthodox Church. According to Samuel "the term 'one' in the 'one incarnate nature of God the Word' cannot legitimately be rendered as the *monos* of the *Monophysites"* (Samuel 2001: 243). The Church as always maintained, from the 6th century to today, not to use the phrase "one nature" in reference to Christ without the phrase "incarnate". So the "one" in the phrase is not a simple one but it is a composite nature of Godhead and manhood as asserted in the Christology of the Syrian Orthodox Church.

In Conclusion, the Christology of the Syrian Orthodox Church is what it teaches in its catechism. This is the summary of its faith. The Syriac Orthodox Church believes in the mystery of

Incarnation. That is, the Only Son of God, the Second Person of the Holy Trinity, took to Himself a body and became man. It further believes that at the time of Annunciation, when the Angel Gabriel was sent to the Virgin Mary, the Holy Spirit came upon her and cleansed her of all-natural impurity, filling her with His grace. Then the Only Son of God came down and entered her immaculate womb, and took to Himself a body through her, thus becoming a perfect Man with a perfect Soul. After nine months, He was born of her and her virginity was maintained contrary to the laws of nature. It further believes that His true Godhead and His true Manhood were in Him essentially united, He being one Lord and one Son, and that after the union took place in Him, He had but one Nature Incarnate, was one Person, had one Will and one Work. This union is marked by being a natural union of persons, free of all separateness, intermixture, confusion, mingling, change and transformation (The Syriac Orthodox Resources-2004).

Chapter 10: General Conclusion:

The principal aim of this paper was to expound the doctrines of the Christology of the Syrian Orthodox Church of Antioch and to show how these are promulgated through its liturgy, especially in the Fraction Rite. Any study of the practices of an ancient Church like the Syrian Orthodox Church must necessarily depend on the unwritten tradition of that Church, as there is not much written material that systematically expresses its faith. The social, political, and religious milieu of the fourth century must be taken into consideration in defining the Christology of the Non-Chalcedonians. The Syrian Orthodox Church, along with other Non-Chalcedonian Churches, closely adhered to the Cyrilline Christology of the unity in Christ, as well as those councils that taught the same dogma of unity (especially the first three Ecumenical Councils). At the Council of Chalcedon, the Alexandrian Churches, under the leadership of Patriarch Dioscoros, could not agree to the formulation of the two natures of Christ. Under the leadership of Patriarch Severus of Antioch, the non-Chalcedonian Churches asserted the Christological positions that stressed the "single" incarnate nature of God the Word, which was thoroughly Cyrilline.

This position was endorsed and propounded by Syrian Church leaders such as St. Ephraim and St. Jacob of Sarug through their hymns and *memres*. This was also a period of greater Hellenic influence on Syriac literature, especially in its liturgy. The St. James liturgy was edited by Moses Bar Kepha, and expanded lists of anaphoras were added to its liturgy. On account of the particularities of the liturgical environment, church fathers such as Mor Jacob and Mor Sarug borrowed from Greek philosophical attitudes to express the faith of the Church in its liturgy. Finally, it was Dionysius Bar Salibi who was able to articulate the faith of the Syrian Church in an expanded order of the fraction in the Syrian Orthodox Church liturgy.

A question which still needs to be addressed is how two great traditions (Chalcedonian and non-Chalcedonian Churches) can find a common ground to address their Christological differences. Perhaps, in spite of 1500 years of anathemas against saints of each group, a union of two parallel traditions is possible based on St. Cyril's Christology. We can look, for example, at the historic statement of reconciliation and unity agreed by Patriarch Cyril of Alexandria and Patriarch John of Antioch in 433 A.D., in which Cyril recognized that the phrase "two natures" could also be used in reference to the divine and human realities in the one Christ. With this historical precedent in mind, the most important first step to achieving unity between the Chalcedonian and non- Chalcedonian Churches is a focus on intra-Orthodox dialogues, perhaps even with a focus on the Christology presented in the Syrian-Orthodox fraction rite. This, in turn might one day lead to Eucharistic intercommunion as an expression of Christ's prayer "that all might be one."

The Final Point.

The purpose of this book is: (1) mainly to build upon the Christological foundation of the Syrian Orthodox Church and an apologetic engagement of how the Christology of the Syrian Orthodox Church relates to the Christology of Church Fathers such as Cyril of Alexandria and Severus of Antioch More importantly, through this book, I hope to establish that the Christology of the Syrian orthodox Church is one and the same of the undivided Church by answering the Christological misunderstanding about the Syrian Orthodox Church's position on the union of two natures of Christ. (2) Secondly, this work will refute the argument that the Syrian Orthodox Church is a Monophysite church and thus reverse the 1400 year old schism resulting from the claim that the Syrian Orthodox Church is a heretic church. Though we cannot change the history, but this study can bring a fresh look on the Christological differences at the Council of Chalcedon. (3) Thirdly, this work will serve as a platform for further readings in the Christological position of the Syrian Orthodox Church and will aid in the ecumenical dialogues between the Oriental Orthodox Churches and the rest of the Christian Churches to establish communion among all churches.

In Conclusion, the theological significance of this work is that, after the Christological controversies in the early Church on the ontological union of Eternal Son and the Incarnation, this study will focus on how the Syrian Orthodox Church understood the expressions "one nature" and "two natures" used by the Church Fathers such as Cyril of Alexandria and Severus of Antioch. The point to be studied further is how the word "physis" was interpreted by Cyril of Alexandria in the Christological formulation and the understanding or misunderstanding of churches at the Council of Chalcedon and thereafter. Moreover, the study will look further at the *Miaphysite* Christology of Cyril of Alexandria and how the faith of the Syrian Orthodox Church formed based on the Christological formulation of Cyril of Alexandria and further interpretation of Severus of Antioch on the "one incarnate nature" of God. This work is looking at the contribution of Severus of Antioch on Cyril's "Hypostasis" and how it contributed to the Christology of the Syrian Orthodox Church.

The practical significance of this work is paramount. Most importantly, this work will show that the Syrian Orthodox Church is not heretical in her Christology. Secondly, there will be an understanding that the Syrian Orthodox Church faithfully maintained the authentic orthodox Christological doctrine and kept the unbroken continuity of the apostolic tradition and ecclesiology. This is most important to have an equal footing on ecumenical dialogue especially with the Eastern Orthodox and Catholic Churches as they set a precondition of maintaining the unbroken apostolic and Christological tradition. I strongly believe this study will help to resolve a major hurdle for church unity, as early churches—Chalcedonian and non-Chalcedonian—proclaimed anathemas against each other. Further, such studies and work will contribute renewed interest in the Christology of the Syrian Orthodox Church among the Western scholars as most of them consider the Syrian Orthodox Church as Monophysite or Eutychian.

Bibliography

Aquinas, Thomas. *Summa Theologica: Complete English Edition in Five Volumes.* Vol. 4. Translated by Fathers of the English Dominican Province. Notre Dame, IN: Christian Classics, 1981.

Barnard, L.W. *Justin Martyr: His Life and Thought.* London: Cambridge University Press, 1967.

Barsoum, Ignatius Aphram. *History of Syriac Literature and Sciences.* Translated by Matti Moosa. Pueblo, CO: Passeggiata Press, 2000.

Bar Kepha, Moses and Georg of the Arabs, *The Book of Life: Two Commentaries on the Jacobite Liturgy,* Translated by R.H. Connolly and H.W. Codrington. Oxford: Williams and Norgate, 1913.

Bar Salibi, Dionysius. *The Commentary of Dionysius Bar Salibi on the Eucharist, Moran Etho-10.* Translated by Baby Varghese. Piscataway, NJ: Gorgias Press, 2011.

Bradshaw, Paul F. *Search for the Origins of Christian Worship*. 2nd ed. New York: Oxford University Press, 2002.

Benni, Cyril Behnam. *The Tradition of the Syriac Church of Antioch*. Translated by J. Gagliardi. London: Burns, Oates & Co., 1871.

Catechism of the Catholic Church. Liguori, MO: Liguori Publications, 1994.

Common Declaration of Pope John Paul II and the Ecumenical Patriarch of Antioch HH Mar Ignatius I Iwas. June 23, 1984. Accessed March 11, 2017. http://w2.vatican.va/content/john-paul-ii/en/speeches/1984/june/documents/hf_jp-ii_spe_19840623_jp-ii-zakka-i.html.

Connolly, R. Hugh. *Didascalia Apostolorum*. Toronto: CrossReach Publications, 2017, Kindle.

Cross, F. L., and E. L. Livingstone, eds. "Apostolic Church Order." In *The Oxford Dictionary of the Christian Church*, 3rd rev. ed. Oxford: Oxford University Press, 2005.

Cyril of Alexandria, *The Letter of Cyril to John of Antioch*, Found in Labbe and Cossart,

Tom.IV., col. 343 and col. 164, ed. Philip Schaff and Henry Wace. The Nicene and Post-Nicene Fathers XIV, Second Series, Albany, OR: Sage Software, 1996.

Cyril of Alexandria. *That Christ is One*. Translated by P.E. Pusey. Ipswich, UK, 1881.

Dara, John. *The Commentary of John of Dara on the Eucharist, Moran Etho-12*. Translated by Baby Varghese. Piscataway, NJ: Gorgias Press, 2011.

Davies, J.G., " Monophysitism." In *The New Westminster Dictionary of Liturgy and Worship,* Philadelphia: The Westminster Press, 1986.

de Lubac, Henri. *The Splendor of the Church*. Translated by Michael Mason. San Francisco: Ignatius Press, 2006.

Denzinger, Henry. *The Sources of Catholic Dogma*. Translated by Roy J. Deferrari. St. Louis, MO: B. Herder Book Co., 1957.

Duchesne, Louis. *Christian Worship, Its Origin and Evolution: A Study of the Latin Liturgy up to the Time of Charlemagne*. London: Society for Promoting Christian Knowledge, 1910.

Etheridge, J.W. *The Syrian Churches: Their Early History, Liturgies, and Literature.* London: Longman, Green, Brown, and Longmans, 1846.

The Coptic Orthodox Church Centre UK "*History of the Coptic Church,*" accessed February 10, 2017, http://www.copticcentre.com/history.

Ignatius of Antioch. *Letter to the Smyrnaeans.* Translated by Cyril C. Richardson. Early Christian Fathers. Grand Rapids, MI: Christian Classics Ethereal Library, 1953.

Jungmann, Josef Andreas. *The Mass of the Roman Rite: Its Origins and Development.* Translated by Francis A. Brunner. Notre Dame, IN: Ave Maria Press, 2012.

Kadavil, Poulose Mor Athanasius. *The Syrian Orthodox Church: Its Religion and Philosophy.* Changanassery, Kerala: Mor Adai Study Centre, 2005.

Kavanagh, Aidan. *On Liturgical Theology.* New York: Pueblo Publishing Company, 1984.

Khalek, Nancy. *Damascus after the Muslim Conquest: Text and Image in Early Islam* New York: Oxford University Press, 2011.

Kollamparampil, Thomas. *Salvation in Christ According to Jacob of Serugh.* Piscataway, NJ: Gorgias Press, 2010.

Madden, Myron. C. *Power to Bless.* New York: Morehouse Publishing, 1999.

Paul, K.P. *The Eucharist Service of the Syrian Jacobite Church of Malabar.* Piscataway, NJ: Gorgias Press, 2003.

Rabo, Michael *The Syriac Chronicle of Michael Rabo (The Great): A Universal History from the Creation.* Translated by Matti Moosa. Teaneck, NJ: Beth Antioch Press, 2014.

Ratzinger, Joseph Cardinal. *The Spirit of the Liturgy.* San Francisco: Ignatius Press, 2000.

Robertson, Ronald "Relations between the Catholic Church and the Oriental Orthodox Churches," Catholic Near East Welfare Association/Resources, accessed on February 1, 2017, http://www.cnewa.org/resources.

Saka, Ishaq. *Commentary on the Liturgy of the Syrian Orthodox Church of Antioch.* Translated by Matti Moosa. Piscataway, NJ: Gorgias Press, 2008.

Samuel, V.C. *The Council of Chalcedon Re-examined*. 2nd ed. Delhi: Indian Society for Promoting Christian Knowledge, 1999.

Schmemann, Alexander. *Introduction to Liturgical Theology*. Translated by Asheleigh Moorhouse. Crestwood, New York: St. Vladimir's Seminary, 1986.

Second Vatican Council. Constitution on the Sacred Liturgy *Sacrosanctum Concilum.*, December 4, 1963. Accessed March 11, 2017.http://www.vatican.va/archive/hist_co uncils/ii_vatican_council/documents/vat-ii_const_19631204_sacrosanctum-concilium_en.html

St Athanasius. *On the Incarnation* Translated and Edited by a Religious of C.S.M.V., Popular Patristic Series-3, Crestwood, NY: St. Vladimir's Seminary Press, 1996.

St. Clement of Alexandria, *The Instructor of the Children*, Translated by William Wilson. From Ante-Nicene Fathers, Vol. 2. Edited by Alexander Roberts, James Donaldson, and A. Cleveland Coxe. Buffalo, NY: Christian Literature Publishing Co., 1885.

St. Cyprian of Carthage. *Epistle to Ephesians.* Translated by Robert Ernest Wallis. From

Ante-Nicene Fathers Vol. 5, Edited by Alexander Roberts, James Donaldson, and A. Cleveland Coxe. Buffalo, NY: Christian Literature Publishing Co., 1886.

St. Cyril of Alexandria, *On the Unity of Christ*, Popular Patristics Series Vol. 13. Translated by John Anthony McGuckin. Yonkers, NY: St. Vladimir's Seminary Press, 2012.

Syriac Orthodox Church: Trilingual Eucharist Service Book. Edited by Kuriakose Corepiscopa Moolayil, 147.Kottayam, Kerala: Mor Adai Study Centre, 2005.

The Book of Common Prayer Book of the Syrian Church. Translated by Bede Griffiths. Piscataway, NJ: Gorgias Press, 2005.

The Martyr, Justin. *The First Apology*, Translated by Cyril C. Richardson. Early Christian Fathers. Grand Rapids, MI: Christian Classics Ethereal Library, 1953.

Torrance, Iain R. *Christology After Chalcedon: Severus of Antioch and Sergius the Monophysite.* Norwich: Canterbury Press, 1988.

Wainwright, Geoffrey, and Karen B. Westerfield Tucker. *The Oxford History of Christian Worship.* New York: Oxford University Press, 2006.

Ware, Timothy. *The Orthodox Church.* Baltimore, MD: Penguin Books, 1963.

Wybrew, Hugh. *The Orthodox Liturgy: The Development of the Eucharistic Liturgy in the Byzantine Rite.* Crestwood, NY: St. Vladimir's Seminary Press, 1990.

Yeldho, Titus. *A Guide to the Holy Qurbono.* Whippany, NJ: MSOSSA, 2012

Youssef, Youhanna Nessim. "Severus of Antioch in the Coptic Liturgical Books." *Journal of Coptic Studies* 6 (2004): 139-148.

Apostolic Constitutions, Book VIII, xiii, in New Advent, last updated 2020.

"General Instruction of the Roman Missal" 151, 180 *The Holy* See, last updated 2010,

Irwin, Kevin W. *Models of the Eucharist.* New York: Paulist Press, 2003. Jesson, Nicholas A. "Les Orandi, lex credendi: Towards a Liturgical Theology." Toronto: Toronto School of Theology, 2001.

Kavanagh, Aiden. *On Liturgical Theology*. Collegeville: Liturgical Press, 1984. Pius XII. *Munificentissimus Deus*. Vatican City: Libreria Editrice Vaticana, 1950.

Prosper Aquitanus. "Praeteritorum Sedis Apostolicae Episcoporum Auctoritates", Capitulum VIII *alias Cap. XI,* in *Patrologiae Cursus Completus (Series Latina 51)*. Edited by Jacques-Paul Migne. Paris, 1861

Thurston, Herbert. "The Elevation", in *The Catholic Encyclopedia*, last updated on 2020.

Varghese, Joseph. "Lex Orandi.mov" at *Sophia University*, last updated on February 8, 2021.

Made in the USA
Columbia, SC
08 February 2025